Rapunzel, Rapunzel

Rapunzel, Rapunzel

poems, prose, and photographs
by women on the subject of hair

edited by Katharyn Machan Aal

 McBooks Press ❧ Ithaca, New York 14850 ❧

Book design by Mary A. Scott
Typesetting by Strehle's Computerized Typesetting
Front cover photograph c. 1900, by Belle Johnson
Back cover photograph by Kathy Morris

Library of Congress Cataloging in Publication

Rapunzel, Rapunzel : poetry, prose, and photographs by women on the subject of hair.
   1. American literature—20th century. 2. Hair—Literary collections. I. Aal, Katharyn Machan, 1952-
PS509.H28R3   810'.8'036   79-28326
ISBN 0-935526-00-5

This book is distributed to the book trade by The Crossing Press, Trumansburg, N.Y. 14886. Individuals may order this book from bookstores or directly from The Crossing Press. Please include $1.00 postage and handling with mail orders.

Printed in the United States of America

2 4 6 8 9 7 5 3 1

To the memory of
Anne Sexton

Contents

Part II: CUTTING

Introduction

Why hair?

The idea for this anthology first came to me two years ago. I realized that the subject of hair was becoming important to me as a feminist issue, and then began remembering how many stories and poems and myths I'd read that dealt with it as a central image. I remembered a creative writing assignment back in 1971 when I was in my first year of college, in which the professor instructed each of us to write a poem about hair after we read Anne Sexton's story, "The Letting Down Of The Hair," and how no one had trouble doing so. And I began to think that there must be others who wrote about and photographed hair. I could easily have compiled an anthology of famous "hair pieces"—from the Bible to any number of twentieth century writers—but what I wanted was contemporary visions of hair, how it is affecting women right now, at the close of the 1970's.

Hair is a true flag of personality and an issue in sexual politics. Women, who from childhood on are taught to respect the importance and sexual value of their "crowning glory," know this fact very well. After all, a radical change in hairstyle is a time-honored symbol of radical inward change. And what of body hair? Here the political line is drawn even more boldly. Legs, underarms, breasts, faces: women today, especially those with dark hair, must shave or depilate or bleach, or run the sure risk of ridicule and even rejection—not only by men who have been conditioned to find female hairiness undesirable, but by other women as well, who perhaps feel threatened by an outward display of independence from the "norm." Women who consciously refuse to comply with custom know that people will notice on **them** the hair that grows, acceptably, in the same places on men.

To my great pleasure, submissions to the anthology poured in from all over the country, convincing me I had been right: hair **is** an important subject to today's women, as a personal concern and as an artistic theme and symbol. The ages of my contributors range from the early teens to the mid-seventies. The following pages exhibit a wide diversity of approaches to the subject of hair, in poems, photographs, short stories, and essays. RAPUNZEL, RAPUNZEL—a celebration of the fascination Anne Sexton understood in this fairy tale, and chronicled so beautifully in TRANSFORMATIONS and THE BOOK OF FOLLY.

Why hair? Because, often dismissed as insignificant and superficial, it is actually an essential part of us, able to represent our inner selves to strangers and friends, able to symbolize important inner changes. We comb it, we cut it, we care for it—and it keeps on growing, as we ourselves do.

Katharyn Machan Aal
May, 1979
Ithaca, New York

11

12

Part I: Combing

BARBARA IN TWO WORLDS
by Joanne Leonard

HAIR

O my wood or orange brush
but not the comb! not the comb!

Phyllis Janik

BRAIDING

One two make them tighter
   you'll never squeeze the curl out.
Even without ribbons
   they slide way down my back.

Cross one, cross over
   Hair so thick
light never catches
   only gets blocked by my lines
in the air

      a mine field

Hair
is wild woman round the edges
snakes skin at the beginning
soft glove leather patting the scalp
rough plastic brushing the skin out

Hair
is a map of years of cells
a glyph   geometry
road map and closet together

Pull your hair away from your ear
if you have any
and I'll whisper a secret about hair:
      it is beautiful a jumbo magic

Rapunzel lived in the tower till the prince
   pulled her down, arranging her golden prison.
Medusa's snakes opened cuts in her throat.
My grandmother was double-process platinum
   till handfuls came out.

Becky Fields at fourteen
taking a piano lesson:
Bad skin, bad teeth.

Bangs taped up over the eyebrows
Her face glued up
like an accident with bubble gum.

First haircut in the family mythology:
  My brother losing curls

The most traumatic:
  My pixie clip at seven.

Tree bark is a more tender protein,
not to mention sperm.

The magic is always implicit.

                    *

One, two you've got to get all the hair in
braids weave a pattern and nothing should
frizz out

The smoothness doesn't appear by magic
you have to work for it
pull the sections even
and make the child stand still

sooner or later they grow too active
but for a while
    the braids are beautiful
the hair young and shiny
calmly ordered.

                              Susan Mernit

WORKS OF ART

Once I've made
The clean white part
It overflows my hands.
Hair in harvest colors:
Gold, orange, red,
Auburn, brown and
Burnt sienna strands.
Hues familiar
Since my childhood paintbox.

Silken soft it spills
And shimmers through my brush,
So rich I can barely work
Its lustrous treasure
With pale and awestruck hands.

Over and under we start.
More and more deftly now
I learn to weave in
The three divisions of your
Small girl braids:
Those themes and elements and times.

Sunshafts dance upon
The rounded final forms
Secure in terminal elastics.
You turn to see my wonder
From knowing patient eyes.
Your old soul tries to tell
What genes, what long ago forebear
Brought you that most unearthly hair.

Ellen Hersh

LEANING DOWN INTO GREEN

safe child is leaning down
into green as if she
knew her way

she has found a flower there
a small black blossom
just at the edge of her fingertips

her golden hair is
melting past her knees
her feet are turning into ivy

her father snaps a summer camera
now she is captured
this is a story saved from sadness

Joyce Odam

RIVERCROSS   Mud falls and grumbles moss.
You believe the water speaks.
Linda Beth, unbraid your hair,
translate the river's song.
Wet rocks push some strange sentence
down the hillside. You catch
one phrase. Girl,
girl with shining hair,
the river runs away.
Snow-felled trunks bridge
banks of halfwords.
The wind speaks another language.
Dialects of leaf and branch
flicker water, Linda Beth.
Ask. Ask the water
where to go.
Peer into its looking glass
and ask, River, what
do you say to me?

Mourning cloaks and swallowtails
flutter like they understand.
Cloudless sky is clear of question.
Linda Beth, turn your head,
your sunshine hair,
so you can read the afternoon,
lessons water teaches sun.

Twilight still hears ripples talk.
Day sets upon your highlight crown.
The river whispers, snow is meltsilk.
Watercress' green roots drown.
Rapunzel after midnight, you smile
your tresses down.
From sky's titan sea
the moon and you
now own three mountains.
Lovely Beth with starlight mane,
at last you know the river's words,
its curls, its waves, and each ringlet.
Its message flows silver
in the silence
of your grandchild's sleep.

Billie Jean James

FOUR VIEWS OF A HAIRBRUSH

In the green shade
of the pink plumaria tree
my daughter
brushes her beachwindwhipped hair
(ninety-two, ninety-three, ninety-four,)
while the birds who own
all the trees around us
talk about her.

The telephone rings.

Her hair, almost shiny soft,
tumbles around her shoulders
as she runs,
and the brush
like a small furrybrown cloud
is left behind
on the lawn.

"How disgusting,"
mutters the old man next door.

I hear him.
But I let it rest,
there by the mint bed, where
Mrs. Mynah Bird is watching,
anxious now
for soft trimmings
for her scratchybrown nest.

Barbara Bown Robinson

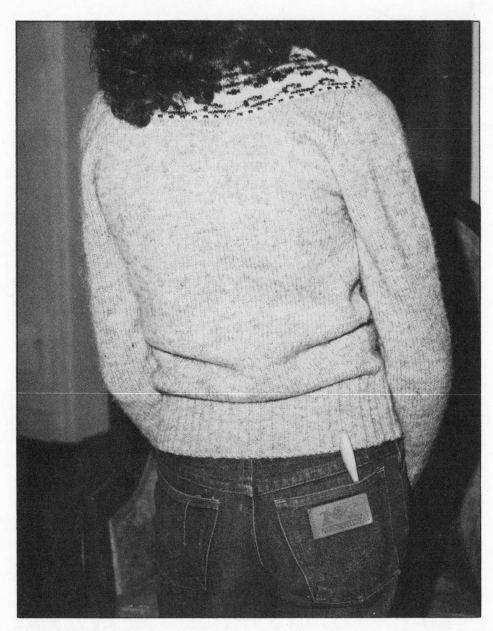

REBECCA KRAMER
by Roger Thorpe

HAIR, THROUGH A SIXTH GRADE POINT OF VIEW

In sixth grade there are various opinions about hair, none of which are a manner of very good taste, except of course my opinions.

Some girls prefer straight hair and others tend to curl their hair which makes it look worse.

Every girl carries a comb in her back pocket which when sticking out causes great temptation to boys.

Every morning there are at least eight girls arranging their hair in the bathroom before school starts. Before my braids were cut my hair was unclassified but my hair is now classified as "frizzy" which is bad; perhaps it's just as well because people like to pull braids.

I was recently at a girlscout slumber party where in the course of one day we brushed our hair four times with about an hour for each brushing.

Whenever somebody cuts their hair, whether it's true or not, they have to say their mother made them cut it.

I have a friend who says my hair would be just beautiful bleached and my grandmother wouldn't like my hair unless it was an inch long (at most).

However frizzy hair may be excused as long as it's well brushed.

Rebecca Kramer

TO MY SISTER, ON HER THIRTEENTH BIRTHDAY

Standing before the mirror, like those
Calico girls, the priggish, prairie lasses
The textbooks do their best to teach
Were your ancestors, putting your hair up.
Till a year ago, you firmly folded it
In plaits each morning, in the same way
You wove camp potholders, made birds
From clay, leafprints with a toothbrush.

At twelve you let it down one day in the park,
And the old men (so melded to their benches
The pigeons treated them as one stone
Configuration) sprang up to watch you pass.
The chinless delivery boys stopped
Still on their bikes, leaving tomatoes
Split on the pavement, sodden strawberries
Cream and Chiclets, running in the gutters.

That spring you wore a blouse with roses
Which caught in your hair. You walked everywhere
With a trail of petals. The street magicians
Sawed you in two, and argued which
Would have the legs, and who the top half
With the miraculous hair. A subway ride
Brought a million midnight proposals. There was
No help for it. You had to put your hair up.

Standing before the mirror, like Seurat's
Bather, whose every point of skin
Is a point of light, putting your hair up.
She lives in a world made private by paint
And canvas, you in this room whose white shade
Keeps out the street, framing you shifting
Between two poses, now lifting your hair up
Stiff and serene, now, letting it down.

                                        Monica Raymond

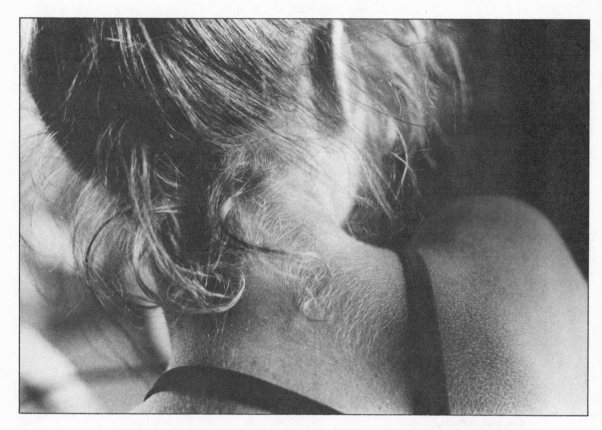

GRETCHEN
by Jan Strausser Kather

MY HAIR

"your hair should be short, full,
not this long hanging."
—hairdresser

My mother agreed
my hair should
puff into curls
for my face long
and my nose
and my olive skin
she framed them all
with collars: peter pan,
ruffled, round platters
of white
to disguise the Mediterranean
length
of my features.

At six
she put me under
a helmet of heat.
My hair held
in metal coils
I waited to flower
like Shirley Temple.

All those years
she kept it cropped
but slowly I began
to let it fall.

And as it grew
I almost thought
what if she's right
waiting for my skin
to turn green
my eyes to bulge
my throat to cackle.

But as my hair
fell beside my cheeks
along my neck
down
down
around my shoulders

down
down
further
till it stroked
my waist
my hips
brushed my thighs
my knees

it swept up
around me
like a cradle
and rocked me.

Rachelle Benveniste

DANCING I
by Kathy Morris

HER HAIR

It was so long she
felt connected to the stars
by it when she washed
she felt the milky way
running through
the strands, dripping
onto her shoulders.

She felt it took
wild journeys
at night
she would dream of stars
there was always
that connection.

Diane Donovan

LYN LIFSHIN

HAIR

in brooklyn one
love's aunt plotted
made an appointment
to have it done
cut in a flip

a present for me
like the scratchy
nylon gowns i
never wore when i
left to marry

an uncle said before
he died he wished
he could see it
short after

the wedding i
pulled pins out of
that stiff hive
for a week afraid
to touch it

when i taught in
highschool i had
to wear it up
sprayed it one
grey morning
with flit as

if it was a
living flying
thing that
shouldn't like
my life seemed
that october

unreal i was
afraid to touch
it all his family
tried to pull it
back into velvet

twist it pin
it choke they said
they wanted to see
my eyes but i
know they suspected
me of being a
hippie a witch

the college that
said i couldn't stay
on white cold paper
wrote first can't you look more
professional and

dignified wear
it up the brother
in law would pull
it sneer ask if i'd
seen the mad

haired girl in
the munsters i
heard that the
whole tv season
later i learned that

what grew out of
the dark where i
couldn't reach
like dreams or
poems was beautiful

shouldn't be
squeezed into
changed into
something different

but those years
apologizing stuffing
that sun bleached red
under my collar

straightening it in
what was ok for the
early sixties and
never letting it
go where it wanted

milkweed wild
flowers poems
animals a dream

hair like someone
who couldn't hadn't
wouldn't admit didn't
know it had a
life of its own

Lyn Lifshin

YOU MUST HAVE BEEN THE DREAM I LEANED ON

Uniform winters, weeks regular
as pleats of my regulation skirt
collecting, as I collected:
fat about my hips, penpals
in Ohio with tacky writing & scrapbooks
on John Lennon, grand designs
to become la jeune chanteuse.

Professional romantic, I let my hair have its way
to my waist, waited for emissaries
in male velvet, their mustaches like glyphs
tasting of whiskey   voices wicked with guitars
strapped to backs fretted with vertebrae
I could say like rosaries, one sure thing
each sun promised to set
before my eyes, while my hair caught in school-
bus doors, fingered the air, a disembodied
scare for homebound traffic, I waited
for a Silvercloud
to find my driveway, leave its tracks, legible,
I was sure & fatal
as the hexagram on my palms.

Alice Fulton

SELF-PORTRAIT
by Alice Fulton

HAIR
(from a series of prose-poems titled SHE)

   she would never cut it. her hair. red. thick.
waves. sensual. long. curled. down. around her breasts.
red. breast curves. the strands curved from her lips.
red. to her nipples. round.
   she washed it. twice. wet. daily. wet. like
her tongue. wet red. wet suds. white shampoo.
white on red. washing red. she dried it. toweled. dry.
vigorous. toweled. dry. her scalp tingled. pulsated.
gratefully.
   she combed it. often. strokingly. lovingly.
often. at her mirror. her hair smiled. red smile.
often. at the office. at parties. often. people. noticed.
men. her hair. she knew it attracted men. her. she was
attracted. to the red. hair. her hair. wavy thick.
thickly red.
   she spoke of it. to it. in front of the mirror.
mirrors. red reflections. spoke softly. to her self.
soothingly. at home. in the shower. to friends.
it was lovely. wasn't it. was it not. they agreed. agreed.
of course. she pet it. softer than cats. fluffy. more
graceful. it grew. gratefully. curled. waved. she
let others touch it. if they could. sensitively.
appreciatively.
   she smelled it. sensually. her nostrils stroked in
the smell. hair smell. red smell. clean. taste smell.
tongue wet red. forbidden smell. she drew in the
smell. sucked red. like other smell wrappers. of
candy bars. lustfully. red smell.
   she would never cut it. never. it was her
life line. her pride. hers only. she parted it.
in the center. perfectly centered. dead center. she
combed it. closer to the center. her eyes saw red. her
nose felt strokes. warm waves. she stroked it. around
her face. lips soft. tongue warm. red cover. she
created her own world. shelter.
red womb.

                              Naomi Rachel

36

BLONDE

He measures her with his eyes,
strokes bare canvas. She is
a porcelain vase, still life
with hair   breasts
legs on a stand he turns
to light. Her eyes
are soft as a lover's
dreaming. In the mirror
the artist's wife gathers
dust, makes the lunch
of cheese omelet, bitter herbs
and scorched green tea.

Ruth Moose

WIG

I
Under the veil
they said
your hair
was as short as
the hair on my hand;
brittle grass
scratched field
a row
of tiny corn.

II
In third grade
she was the one
who made you kiss
your comic good-bye
if she caught it
in your lap.
Her white face
framed
by whiter linen and one
black strand
we would ask
to go to the bathroom
just to get close enough
to see.

III
I never questioned the moustache
thought only
it had replaced the brows;
become
lowered.

It was the brown mole
fat as sin
(it waved when you talked)
I did not
understand.

IV
Spring brought the changes;
legs we never believed in
sprouted like roots—
skirts rose with the grass,
veils shortened
and like mold
on a new-thawed lawn
each face
grew bangs, a tendril
near the ear, a soft wave or
pinned curl.
We wondered
why a blonde nun
had ever become
a nun
at all.

V
One month
after the scandal
you arrived
at my home. Your hair
was a black flag
at your back—it must have
been growing for months—watered
each night, held under
the beam of a votive candle.

"This is my sister-in-law,"
you said,
throwing the hair off your
shoulders.

I smiled,
reached out
and kissed
your brow.

Karen Marie Christa Minns

MARGEDDA'S HAIR
(an excerpt from THE MOTHERLORDS)

Margedda's hair is the crest of a male bird at the height of the mating season, the season of show-off. Things do not go into her hair so much as they appear constantly to be popping out of it—long rods of metal, huge wooden or tortoise-shell combs, intricate gold panoramas suspended on stilts walk about easily in Margedda's hair, which is also like the sea in a beautiful storm; Margedda's dangerous hair. It rises and foams and ebbs, forms caves plains peaks and tendrils that drip down her neck and the fronts of her ears like simple vines. In its many forms it changes by the hour, extending herself so far in any direction that to imagine Margedda without her hair is like imagining someone else without a face. Margedda's hair is horns and antlers, mane, crest and peacock tail, elephant ears, and cities seen from a great distance. Nothing extraneous to her comes near it, out of respect; it is not meant for touching, it is for the eyes to see what they dare; the hands could learn nothing from it. Margedda's hair speaks of what is possible, and what is not. She makes of it an organic sculpture, careful as if it were granite and could only be done once, temporary as a one day moth. Nothing can change Margedda's hair, change is its only name, incorporating wind and straw, dust and rain into its body, giving them a meaning they would never think of themselves, without Margedda. Into the city of her hair Margedda plants red and orange flares, rubies and golden stones; her hair is a night lit with many fires; amber stones carved as tiny figures holding tiny mirrors of gold flakes reflecting tiny red stones live next to tall copper storks or brass bells, hollow with more metal cast inside to make a clattering sound. Margedda's love of brass has caused her to be called a brazen woman; never would she think of leaving her hair naked or soundless except to create the magic of nakedness. She washes some of her hair at a time but never all of it and never does she wear more things in it than have meaning. Margedda can be very simple when it is a simple day, but looking into Margedda's hair especially if anyone is concentrating, is to see the many wonders of your own mind and the transformations of your life. Since this can be dangerous, everyone uses Margedda's hair with precision and thoughtfulness.

Judy Grahn

SPRING COMES TO SENECA STREET

for Katharyn and Bill

They sit on the porch steps
watching other people climb
towards a perfect sky
over Fontana's Shoe Store
at the top of the hill

Slowly he combs her hair
drying in sunlight
over and over   his arm bends
her hair swept soft as the newest crocus
by the faded garage

Always the arc of his arm
her hair the strangers leaning uphill
flawlessly balanced against gravity
the sun   the bluest sky

Beverly Tanenhaus

JEWISH WIFE

When Risa crosses her long legs
the length of her
a lovely shyness on the couch ·
softens all the corners in the room

but when she lets down
her kerchiefed hair
all the wadis of Judea go streaming
in the rush of spring

                    Marcia Falk

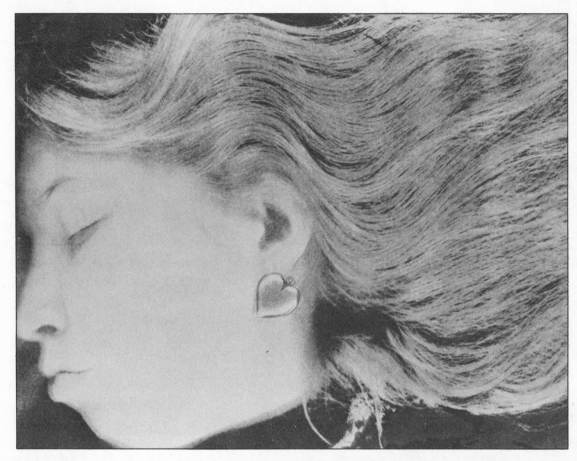

SELF-PORTRAIT AS SLEEPING BEAUTY
by Jacqueline Livingston

HAIKU #35

The comb glides through my
hair, I think of my husband
fishing the river.

Conciere Taylor

WOMAN COMBING

> "   It must
> Be the finding of a satisfaction, and may
> Be of a man skating, a woman dancing, a woman
> Combing. The poem of the act of the mind."
>   —Wallace Stevens

I should braid, tie back, bind this hair away
from you, but drawing half over each breast
I let the strands merge and fall like the manes
in a Clairol commercial. You tangle
and snarl my hair, with hands that mean
to fit things in place. And you say
I try too hard to be Rapunzel.

The first day to imagine spring,
I bent my head to the wind—comb, jerk
and pull through the mats on the back of my neck.
A handful ripped from the scalp,
and now my lines are again certain,
unwavering from crown to waist.
The mass of knots and snarl released
to the air, it bumps on shingles,
catches on the gutter. The sparrows fly by;
it is too confused for their nest.

Two days of bobbing on the rainspout,
and the tangle pulls free. I see it in the wind,
but the breeze dies, and my discarded hair falls
to the street. Bumping like a tumbleweed, it clings
to the wheel of a bicycle. I think
I see it whirling on a spoke.

                                    Kathleene West

AFTER A MILLION STROKES

It is you I see at night,
standing beside me in the mirror.

We are brushing our hair,
long
over our shoulders.
The windows are open only a fingernail.
You, more willing to stand the heat
than hayfever.
I not wanting to smell
the night steeped in the pickle factory.
Our elbows touch occasionally.

You tell me you put your extra shoes
in a long box under your bed.
I say I keep mine out
where I can see what choices I have.

We are in bed,
the lights have been out only minutes.
And I see your newly plaited braids
tucked neatly around your ears,
the ends, curling
above your breasts.
My shoes slither under the door
and the bedspread starts to unroll at my feet.
My hair sizzles.

You are sleeping.

Barbara Somers

SOMETHING IN THE WINGS, THE VINES

Locked away by uncles, husbands,
in castle wings, in damp regions,
they were allowed the parapet, the garden,
their maids and their musicians.
Still, how did they break up the days
which grew heavier than brocade or crowns
or the shafts that pierced their hangings
around the bed in the morning?

Prayer took time, but the tongue wandered
and the knees grew numb. In the garden
the rows of clanking men
stifled a quickened breathing,
the circling of the fountain.

They could eat marzipan,
needlework abandoned
and laps seeded with crumbs,
till their heads rolled sideways
and the lute players crept away
with reddened fingers.
They could go to bed with ankles swollen
and stay there till their hair
fell out in clumps
and their skin grew yellow as muslin.

But surely some,
shedding an old gown,
discovered the skin that had been
trapped in a fencing of titters and fans.
Ah, then the words of ballads
flicked up through them
till their closed lids pulsed
like pregnant bellies
and they played with their maid's fingers.
Ah, then the morning was light
as the ropes of hair
they braided for their maid
singing songs to its color
and to the birds that wove
the strands they gave them.

For them rooms sometimes shone,
and it was more than sun
or wind coming down chimneys
to fan embers.
Sometimes faces shone
and it was more than rain
on the parapets where they would lean
with flapping cloaks thrown open,
till something in the tapestries
they labored on
made the warden wonder,
something in the wings, the vines.

Sybil Smith

ANNE SEXTON'S RAPUNZEL

Again I cast my hair
down to the grass, the crowds
applauding each golden thread
that spins into their dreams.
They come each day
to see the rainbow show,
the sun tilting past my tower
to perform for them through me.
Each morning, the same ritual:
the soaping,
the rinsing,
the hanging out to dry. Gradually

I have become a world wonder,
object of legend
and the clicking of black cameras.
For the tourists I am
goddess, princess,
and my yellow tresses
a ladder to forever. They see me
taken by a charming prince
with arms strong as their fantasies,
his face brave and eager, his mouth
impatient to press against me
and free me from the stone walls
of my flesh. Once again I smile.
Today as every day

I gaze into a glowing sky
where clouds dance one by one
and the wind makes music on a single flute.
Those who gather below
see me wistful, combing vainly
for the man who will surely come.
Their hopes cannot accept my happiness;
my solitude offends them. I say
nothing, knowing it would do no good,
would only set them muttering
rumors of madness, threats of expulsion.
They will never understand:

my smile is real, my tower is beautiful,
my hair hangs down for me alone,
a rope that will defy any prince.

Katharyn Machan Aal

HAIR

beowulf's widow let
hers flow loose
when her husband
died like some mid
west plains indians
flowing wild like
grass like grief
the braid of the
dead man cut from
the corpse put in
a sacred bundle
with braids of his
other dead family
carried by his
woman when she'd
move like the hair
wreathes in new
england 50 years
of a gone family
braided together
under glass locked
and hung over the
fire as a painting
some photo grabbed
running in the
snow with the guns
the drums coming

                              Lyn Lifshin

JANE

"...was she a frontier Florence Nightingale, Indian fighter,
army scout, gold miner, pony express rider, and stagecoach
driver? Or merely a camp follower, prostitute, and alcoholic?
Was her father a farmer, gambler, army sergeant or minister?
Her birthplace Illinois, Missouri, or Fort Laramie?"

—WILD MEN OF THE WILD WEST

Let's start with her
at Fort Laramie. **Sources agree**
she was fond of blue blouses, brass buttons;
agree to her black eyes at 15, black curls
cut short; at 28, brown eyes, brown tresses;
at 32, flaming red hair blowing in all directions.

So she poses
(in beaded buckskin, blue flannel shirt,
wide-brimmed felt hat
astride a yellow pony,
Winchester & revolver & cartridge belt
& fluid ammunition in the saddle bags)
a problem for biographers.

How did she get her name?

While Bronco Moll
and Virginia, the wife of Wild Man Jack Slade,
wore short skirts and a pair
of silver-plated derringers
slung to a rattlesnake belt around their waists;

while Madame Mustache dealt twenty-one;
while sage hens Rocking Chair Emma
Poker Alice Scarface Annie & Rowdy Kate
followed the Wild West
trails on to Tombstone;

benevolent women in Deadwood
would teach Calamity sewing, maybe
see her a dressmaker

but swaggering with her bull whip
at the opening of the Gem Variety Theater
it is said she danced
in a Stetson & purple silk neckerchief,
danced with the girls and led them
to the bar for drinks.

How did she get her name?
It seems most likely
she had good teeth and heart
could pack a horse or mule and throw
the diamond hitch
could ride a bucking bronco
was no mean revolver shot
chewed long cut & plug
and saved Antelope Frank from the Indians.

She outlived Belle Starr,
outlived Hickok by 27 years to the day
—said Boys, bury me next to Wild Bill
(actually there is no legal proof
of this marriage).

How did she get her name?
She celebrated making sport.
She learned by heart
the story of her life.

Brave men married her,
swearing toward the end
they'd married calamity indeed.
Indians called her crazy woman,
watched not far from her campfires,
admired her black horse they called devil horse

and **this document has not been generally accepted** but
unmolested, Calamity Jane at 32 rode through
the Sioux camps standing on her head,
wisps of golden cotton-fine at her temples;
brown strands like buffalo grass in the wind;
waves or falls like shocks
of dark fireweed; her
flaming red hair blowing in all directions.

Phyllis Janik

GROWING UP, GROWING OUT

And now,
my head is like
a proud November woods:
the ice and snow glint sharply
against the russet leaves.

Why dye? Because we live in a youth-crazed society, I imagine. Aging, maturing, growing polished like fine wood is not looked on as a positive goal in our culture.

I started to go grey in my twenties, and didn't think much about it. I was tangled in a bad marriage, had a small child to care for, and was desperately looking for direction in my life. One day, during an intense discussion, my best friend's boyfriend blurted out, "You know, if you'd lose ten pounds, dump your husband, and dye your hair—you're too young to go grey; life's too short to keep going on this way—everything will turn out right." Too simple? Too talismatic? Maybe. The first and last steps were fairly easy; however, I didn't realize when I started dyeing my hair how permanent a move it was to be, or the consequences and hidden dangers of hair dyes. The middle step took longer; some things don't die quickly. (. . . we separate as long and slow/as two old caramels/stick in summer—/the long ends messy,/trail off in the breeze. . . .)

But now I had a new image: slender, my hair long and glossy brown, and a new life. I started writing. It had threatened my first husband, so I had put it off. I can't imagine ever doing that now, having "boarded the train there's no getting off" (Plath). I went back to graduate school to get my Masters in English. At the same time, I started teaching English in a nearby college, part-time, as I still had a three-year-old to care for. I found this was the first job I'd ever had that I really **liked** going to. (I'd been a waitress, postal employee, Civil Service Examiner, etc.) I got involved with sports, after leading a sedentary life. I got into tennis, skiing, hiking, camping, and canoeing. I started dating. I was flying, my long hair shining.

It is interesting to see how superficial changes (hair, dress, weight loss) can precipitate deeper, more meaningful ones, and, conversely, how these same surface changes can be dismissed if they don't fit in with the new identity after it is fully formed.

For me, happy as I was with my "new" color, which was my regular color minus the grey and plus shine and highlights, I was not happy with the process itself, which was very messy, or with the fact that hair dyeing is phony and unnatural, an antithesis to the new, outdoorsy me. As a feminist, I wondered if hair dyeing wasn't part of the old "woman-as-idol" stereotype. Then I read an article in **Ms.** which stated that researchers had found that hair dyes could cause birth defects. We (I was happily remarried now) were considering a baby, and once we had made up our minds, I decided to let my hair grow out.

Another factor that influenced my decision was that during a poetry workshop I announced that it was my 31st birthday and found that everyone had looked on me as 21 or so. Most of the poetry that I write would seem superficial and flighty coming from a younger person. I've done my dues. I see these silver hairs unwinding, and it's part of the cycle. Would spring mean as much without winter?

Recently, too, researchers are finding that hair dyes cause cancer. I wonder if there'll be a new blooming of shining grey heads as a result?

Growing out was a positive time for me, since it was the result of a conscious decision, a choice. I found a hairdresser who agreed with me, and who gave me a good, shorter cut that helped minimize the striped effect of my hair. The part of my hair that had been colored had also become bleached by the sun, creating a charming effect of dark brown/grey hair on top and light brown to reddish hair on the bottom. However, after a few months, the line of demarcation became less evident, and the colors blended in. It's been a year now, and it's still not all grown out.

Friends' reactions have ranged from enthusiastic to strange. I asked a male friend, whom I hadn't seen in months, if he'd noticed I was letting my hair grow out. "I certainly did," was his reply. If I were insecure, I would have headed back to hit the dye bottle. But I like all of the new me—my life with Richard, my teaching and writing, my involvement with sports and the outdoors, and my children, including and especially this one to come. And my hair is a part of it, and me. I don't like dresses and makeup; I like my jeans and streaked-out hair. "Hate that grey/Wash it away" and "Only her hairdresser knows for sure" have become ironic, anti-feminist slogans. As for me—I'm grey and I'm proud!

Barbara Crooker

THE INHERITANCE

I've learned to accept the medical diagnosis:
female-pattern alopecia, a hereditary disorder.

If I live to marvel at my eightieth birthday
baby-pink scalp will shamelessly shine
through silky strands of fine white hair.

But if passing years can somehow transform me
into a woman worn bald with wisdom,
dignified & lovable despite eccentricity,
I'll proudly wear my glossy-headed legacy
in memory of my maternal grandmother.

Born to an age of braids & ribbons,
afflicted in every bone of her skull
by the pain of Victorian women,
my grandmother combed & knotted her losses.

Joanne Seltzer

EIGHTY-EIGHT

Eighty-eight—
she said she was
losing her hair
at last it was
long and flowing
like a comet
white against
the blackness coming.

At this time she was
used to becoming
less: only her hair
reminded her of
Spanish princess back
ground inside
she still danced
when she heard Greek
music: the violins
straightened her;
her toes tapped
time with her cane.

Eighty-eight
she couldn't believe
she was losing—

no more the raven—
but then white
suited her better. She
supposed it to be
color of ermine cloak
it was better than being
naked and losing
all the wrappings.

Diane Donovan

DEAD WOMEN

return
to brush
their hair.

They use our combs,
careful not to break
the teeth.

They borrow our brushes,
leaving a trace of hair
in the bristles.

They enter our beds
to feel the warmth of a man
they have almost forgotten,

but not forgotten.
They try on our gloves and soft
scarves.

They try on our nightgowns
and turn slowly
in front of the mirror.

In the morning we wake,
smooth out the gowns and scarves
in the drawer, sit in front

of the mirror.
We raise the brush or comb to our heads,
stop, notice the hair,

continue.

Siv Cedering Fox

Part II: Cutting

photo by Barbara Adams

RAPUNZEL

I know now
that parents do not die.
They go down the street
to dine on rampion,
binding me to a witch
who keeps me here
clearing their attic.

My hair graying, breaking
too brittle to be a ladder
I let down instead these lines
spinning three truths.

I have found a truth
about the prince—
hair won't hold him.
He will feel the thorns,
grow older, need bifocals.
From this attic
I imagine him, straying.

I have found a truth
about the witch—
she and I are one woman.
Imprisoned by my own past
each day I grow more ruthless
discarding the family trappings
yet more eccentric wanting to save
all snippets of my youthful life.

And I am finding
a truth about scissors—
cutting presages wholeness.
I could stay here forever
tracing yellowed words on old paper
never making my way to the ground
or cut loose and be consumed
like hair, like rampion.

Kathryn Christenson

AFTER BERNICE BOBBED HER HAIR

she went back to Eau Claire
(they said, that snip . . .) but a girl
can make it there, let me tell you.
Scott Fitzgerald was not the first
to send a woman running from
Saint Paul.
                It's true
her father was shocked,
said a shorn lamb was no better
than a black sheep, but
all the girls in Eau Claire
never having seen Summit Avenue
wanted to look just like Bernice.
Her mother slipped her five years'
allowance in advance. She leased
a shop, learned marcels
and finger waves, learned a woman
can fall in love with a scissors.
Daily she voiced the Saint Paul line
and kept her real thoughts private.

She built a little empire
on shears, talk and curling machines.
After the Second War she retired
but gave home permanents
to us girls in the neighborhood
while our polish hardened.

Zelda burned, and cousin Marjorie
blazed out on Summit Avenue.
Bernice lives yet in Eau Claire
a fading flapper on Medicare
still nicknamed "Bobbie" for her hair
shortened by a first girlish dare.

                          Kathryn Christenson

PROTECTING MYSELF

My hair was always
cut above my ears
and shaved in the back
by a bald man
who hummed and grunted.

Old Moon Skull,
man of my nightmares—
he entered with my mother,
her head covered
with thin black snakes.

I threw a lit match
and the snakes went wild,
biting her chin and nose.
And the flames rose—
so many gold tongues.

When I saw Old Moon Skull
he was burning,
but I was safe
beneath my hair,
a lake of blonde water.

                          Lucille Day

A HARVEST OF UNICORNS

there are pictures
i've seen them
fluttering down
the memory tube
disposed   gone
but i saw

sometimes i can
catch these images
falling past
my internal retina
fix them sharply
into focus

my brother
had blond curls
haloes of honey and silk

while my mother
stood jerking his stroller
back and forth
in the winter-steamed bakery
the ham-armed women
clucked at him
patted his honeyed head
and said:
such a beautiful girl

such a beautiful girl
as she waited number-in-hand
at the meat market

such a beautiful girl
as she pushed him
up and down the iced streets

such a beautiful girl
sitting in her woolened lap
on the unheated bus

dammit   my mother said
to the barber with his head

my brother sat in the special horse-chair
supposed to help little boys
forget about their hair
only my brother didn't
bucking on the plastic horse
ducking the sharp scissors

the barber ended up swearing too

my brother hiccuped his sobs all the way home

but my mother wasn't done
this was her only male child
the only son

she took out my old
brown high chair, his now
and just waited a bit
for my brother to forget

she swooped down
roping him into her arms
leading him neat and snug
into the chair
and began to cut
all that honeyed hair
herself

he didn't cry as much
or toss his head wildly
like a scared pony
he just cried a little
and hung his head a lot

my mother swept up the curls
her broom brushing across
the swirled blue linoleum
a tide of tiny unicorns
into the dustpan

my mother flung her head back
proud
her nostrils flaring
like she'd just won a race

Christina V. Pacosz

TWO RED-HEADED FABLES

1.
Mary Lou's beautiful
long red hair
twisted in the chains
of the swing
her face wrinkled and red
like an angry baby
she never expected pain
when she began her dizzy whirl
the world a green blur
smelling of April

she was older than we were
brave and already bearing
breasts like pieces of armour
we stood amazed
at her helplessness
and waited agape
while her mother
untangled the copper
strands from the
iron links

2.
Diana lived up the street
in the low red house
on the corner.
She was the prettiest girl
in the eighth grade.
Her red hair reached her waist.

The admiring younger girls played
beneath the willow tree
in her front yard.
Its branches reached the ground.
The shelter they made
was a green fairy palace
and Diana was the queen.

When Diana was seventeen
she cut her Rapunzel hair
to be in style, to look older.
Her red curls lay dead
on the cold linoleum
of the beauty salon.

That same year, in the fall,
Diana's father cut down the Willow.
He told us it was blighted and dying
and that we shouldn't be sad.
But as we grow older
and learn to make connections
the world seems drained of color.

                    Jennifer Kidney

HAIR IN THE WIND

My hair when I run
                When I bike
            When I stand in down-drafts from towers
Hair my red-grass hair
            Is a banner to the wind
The waves take my hair in mermaid floats

My hair folds me into sleep
            Keeps me warm in winter
                    No need for a cap of wool
Ninety degree days I pile it up against sweat
            My Father balding even in his college pictures
I was his triumph of hair
            How red in the lamplight he would say
                    Like Venetian glass

Curled to my waist in child days
            While I practised the piano in early-morning snows
Mama would brush my hair round her finger
                    To reluctant curl
One day she said I could cut it to fashion
            Ran home to hear Papa's praise
                    But he was a thunderstorm
I tried to grow my curls back
            But they would flower only to my shoulders
Through the years I would tease him
            Now do you forgive me
He died without saying I forgive
            And now I guess he never will

Hostess hair   warm and welcoming
            Don't know the delight of taking it down from a coif
                    For my love
It has never been coifed

My hair   the flowering of my stalk
            I washed my hair by Loch Lommond
Waded out to dry it on a rock
            Running my fingers through the red-grass tangles
                    In the Scottish sun of my ancestors
            Papa watching from the balcony

                                        Emilie Glen

66

HAIR

she was always so beautiful my mother blond she was and
    fair with eyes that turned from green to grey and back
again to green. for her a girlchild should have been like
    that with long blond hair that she could braid and curl and
fix with ribbons. not like me. me with tight black curls, like
    a pickaninny she said. or did I only think she said that.
in my daydreams I was always running and my hair was flying in
    the wind long and black straight and shining. My daughter
says to me 'mommy, how come when you shake your head, your
    hair doesn't move?'   she tried everything my mother fine
tooth combs heavy black brushes beauticians of every
    persuasion. still my hair curled and curled like my
father's coarse and black why was it so important? once when
    I was sick she braided it for me I looked like Topsy . . .
ponytails pigtails pageboys flips these were my earliest
    deprivations. when I was 21 she was vindicated. on west 57th
street a funny little man from Hungary straightened my hair for
    an exorbitant fee. everyone said   I looked wonderful. I was
married in white   and long straight hair. the funny little
    hungarian gave me a hairbrush for a wedding present.
my husband and I in a fifth floor walk-up could not afford
    straight hair.   on 72nd street in a hotel with an english
name a woman called Ila cut my hair. clucking her tongue she
    scolded me, 'imagine   hiding all those lovely curls'.
suddenly I was in vogue. it was chic to sport an afro.
    everyone said I was lucky. I bought my first afro comb and
no one looked at me funny. a strange feeling for me to be in
    fashion. (why did it ever matter?) for many years my
mother and I fought a war over hair. my mother struggled as
    with an enemy.   only now I understand it was never me.

Gail Kadison Golden

ROBIN BECKER
by Jane Kogan

PHONE CALL AT 1 AM

for Debbie

You're still giving me the same line about how you'll be one of
the best painters in NYC in 10 years. For a year you've told
me that your kitchen's almost finished. Meanwhile you eat at
the corner, at work, at the place across the street. You've
ruined another painting. You say you didn't know when to
stop. I think of all the poems that die, turn hard & brittle once
the effort is over. You hate to admit anything's over. That
summer, I lost my watch & you believed it would turn up.
When you lost your glasses at the river, I laughed. Now you
explain why you haven't written, what snagged you in my
letter. I imagine you reading, ready with a pencil to argue in
the margins. Tracklights remind me of you, & the smell of
turpentine; black turtlenecks & haircuts that end in perfect
triangles, as if the shape would last forever.

Robin Becker

CAMOUFLAGE

to each black-
haired woman
with hazel-green
eyes
i reveal
my magical secret

dye yr hair
the color
of the earth

yr eyes
will pick up
the tint
from yr hair
& change
to respectable
concealing
brown

so that none
can guess
yr name—
accurst
creature
from the middle
ages

in drab disguise
you might be able
to postpone
a while longer
yr last debt
to the red-beard
devil

who will sift
yr ashes
from the stake
tomorrow

Joanne Seltzer

SHE AWAITS HIS WRATH

How to explain to him the long
fuchsia dress with
embroidery at your breast was your
two weeks' salary, and

the woman you sketched across
his sketch of you, and worst
of all your hair—your hair

swept from your sister's kitchen
floor, asleep in a brown
bag, waiting to grow a new head.
The night will be

long, and full of hard faces.
It rattles its dice
in your bones' cups.

But if you could say your morning's eyes
saw death without rope or
gun, your prescriptions empty, then
why not dance joy that the corpse

walks, is warm and still
hot to his arms, why not
love this new woman who's
been out all day saving lives?

Wendy Tȳg Battin

OLLIE FRANCES' SILVER BRAID

you said
you said that
I know what
you said you would
never I know
you said you would
never let them
cut your hair no one
not even that cousin
juanita in corpus christi
not let her cut
and perm and
blue and send
you off to
be a real
old lady you had that
hair steel gray
still strong hands
would take
down and braid up
at night
once a week
you sweetly ask me
stick these pink sponges
in twist them
so I do harder
than necessary
when you wince
but don't speak
I do it again
want to scream
stupid old
lady why don't you
go away
let the other one
come back

Carol Fewell

HAIR

Ardently down the backs of cousins
in Poland until it brushed their ribs
the silkworm cousins grew the hair
Sarah Fishoff Silverman peddled
in Missouri.
In Sedalia meager enterprising waves
swelled over coils and switches
off Polish Jews, hair grown
to drape on Sarah's forearm.
She walked the town selling hair
of those who stayed behind,
sticking her other palm out with coins,
trusting strangers to make change
for the hair that caught the fancy
of stylish Midwestern ladies,
the curls and braids that pleased the Nazis
who trimmed their lampshades with Jewish hair,
fashioned bellcords to summon butlers
from my cousins' hair that grew no more.

Maxine Silverman

AT AUSCHWITZ

they cut our hair
great bins of hair
from every head and torso
for cleanliness they said

and my hair
long sleek   black
the hair I loved to brush
to let spill over my shoulders
like a cloak enfolding me
within myself

I am no longer woman
no longer female
I am raped deflowered
for cleanliness they said

it is now i am unclean
besmirched degraded
a stripped nothing feeling
more bald more naked
than at birth
because i have known covering
the identity it gave

                    Thelma Scarce

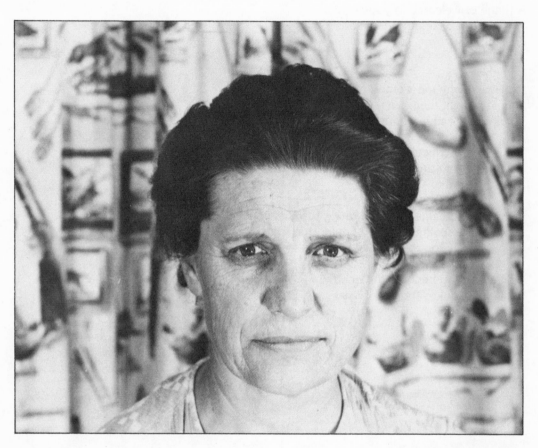

THELMA SCARCE
by Chester Scarce

MY HAIR IS BLACK

Yesterday you were kind, a new breed
Of man I would believe in; your beard
A fringe of welcome to your lips,
Your tongue asking no questions
I could not answer.

You, the rabbi,
Explaining why the women
Should not cut their hair
To please the men in prayer shawls.

This was a sacrifice
Unnecessary to understand the Torah,
A brutal route to God.

Last night I dreamed I was running towards you
Slowly black feathers floated behind me Black feathers
Mounding my footsteps   Black feathers

How easily you become the enemy.
How ugly I look without my hair.

                          Beverly Tanenhaus

HAIR   My first memory is when I am under two years of age, and I am
looking into the full-length mirror in the hall of our two
story house in Kansas City. My mother has taken me to get a
haircut. I hate it. I cry. I am so upset that my mother lets
me grow my hair until I am six.

I had two big, brown, bushy ponytails. There is a picture of me
and my brother holding the tiny fish we have caught. I have two
upper teeth missing and bangs and a plaid shirt and navy blue shorts.
I am wonderful, with my wavy hair.

But she cut it, because the fashion was for short hair and skirts
almost to the ankles. She permanented it while I fought the
nausea and tears. One inch bangs crinkled up and made me look
like a poodle.

In high school I had the Mia Farrow haircut. Way before anyone
had heard of Mia Farrow. It was called the "pixie". I think my
mom just liked the name. After all, I was the shortest kid in my
class. "Leprechaun" would have been more like it.

I envied, oh, how I envied Mary Kate Sawaki. The girl in acappella
chorus with the long blond ponytail. One day she came to class with
bangs. Her hair was receding, she said, from being pulled back tight,
with rubber bands. I didn't care. I would have risked it. She
had a boyfriend in college, she conducted the orchestra.

When I went to college I grew my hair. But shore it off when my
boyfriend left to go to Brazil. It grew back.

After I married, my husband said I looked like a hippie. I had
taken to wearing my long hair in a braid to remind him of home, of
his Indian heritage. I cut my hair to shoulder length and rolled it.
He was proud of me.

When I left him, I cut my hair in a shag. I felt like a dog with
the wrong fur on. I let it grow and grow. It gets tangles in it.
I sit in front of the television some nights and tear clumps full
of rat's nests out. It takes half an hour to wash and about two
days to fully dry.

Sometimes I dream about someone with scissors sneaking up behind
me, who cuts off my hair. I scream and scream. It's my beauty,
it's my river of longing, it's my fish on the line, I caught it
                                            myself.

Paula Inwood

THE SHORT HAIR

It is time to
let down your hair now.
He is waiting below
with his arms full of tremble
and you are so far away,
so unobtainable.

Look,
he is pacing the earth,
a frustrated lover.
He will soon be angry.
He will accuse you.

Rapunzel (if that is your name)
be kind to him.
You are too bright for towers.

Whisper to him to be patient,
you are doing the best you can. . .

but when you were bored,
when you were fed up,
when you were self-vindictive
and being a martyr. . .

ah,
there were those
sharp and shining scissors. . .

Joyce Odam

YOUR UNCLE WILL DIED TODAY

Linda Sellers Peavy

"Your Uncle Will died today. Heart attack at seventy."

Long after her mother's "goodbye," Jana finally realized she was still holding the telephone receiver. As she moved to replace it, her mind cruelly juxtaposed the letter she'd always intended to write against the news she had just received. Uncle Will, dead at seventy. Uncle Will, beloved renegade among the born-agains, the only accepted family member known to drink, swear and tell dirty jokes. Uncle Will, the laughing, loud-mouthed bachelor she had wanted so to please.

"Where's 'Theme Song'?" his booming voice came back as clearly here in her dorm room as it had those many years ago on the farm. Hearing the hated nickname, Jana had always cringed; yet loving the man who gave it to her, she had never failed to come out of hiding to receive his mingled praise and damnation.

"Theme Song," a Dick Tracy comic strip character whose frazzled hair and unkempt appearance became a national joke, seemed an apt enough title for a tomboy whose hair was more often adorned by wisps of hay or pine needles than by velvet ribbons.

It wasn't that the grownups hadn't tried to give her naturally straight and unruly hair the Shirley Temple image which a devoted uncle had every right to expect of his favorite niece. During agonizing Sunday morning sessions, those who cared attacked the week's accumulation of stubborn rat's nest tangles, twisting the hair around sharp-bristled brushes until it fell in loose ringlets Grammy proudly declared "almost as lovely as Cousin Vanessa's."

The miracle workers need not have bothered. For Jana, hair was only fun when it was free, and once not even then. During a summer afternoon's blissful spin in a madly twirling swing, her flying, shoulder-length hair had been caught up by the twisting ropes, hair and hemp forming a gruesome, scalp-jerking plait. Absalom fashion, she'd hung screaming until horrified mother and grandmother came running to her rescue.

Frantically, ineffectively, the two women tried to set her loose by pulling the hair free strand by strand. With each effort, her terror and the volume of her screams intensified. Hearing her wails at last, Uncle Will, home on his yearly visit, burst out of the house with a thundered, "Hell, Nettie, you're torturing the girl! Get me some scissors!"

As the woman meekly obeyed, the big man knelt on the hard-packed ground beneath the swing and put his arms around her. Firmly, yet gently, he urged, "Theme Song, hush up that crying now and hold still for me. I can't cut you loose if you wiggle so." Over and over he coaxed, "Hush, hush and rest easy. Your Uncle Will is here."

At his touch, her wild flailing diminished. Frantic screams dissolved into whimpers. She relaxed, hypnotized by his presence. Carefully, deliberately, he snipped away at her tangled ringlets, whispering words of encouragement and ignoring the horrified gasps of Mother and Grammy. "There. You're free," he announced at last. Filled with relief and gratitude and unable to restrain her feelings any longer, Jana fell into his arms, heaving great, deep sobs of relief.

"There, there, Theme Song. You're okay now," he comforted, holding her close as he rocked back and forth on his knees.

"But her lovely curls . . .," Grammy began.

"Tarnation, woman! You and Nettie would have torn her scalp off to save those damned curls. Leave her alone now. The hair will grow back soon enough."

He was right, of course, but it grew back straight, not in ringlets. The women all shook their heads and clucked their tongues, lamenting the loss of her beauty. Then, without any warning to Jana, though the move was obviously premeditated, her Mama announced. "Christine Parmley is coming by this morning. She just gave herself one of those new-fangled home permanents and has bought one for you. She's real good at it. Your curls will be back in no time."

Trapped. And this time Uncle Will was safely home in Memphis, unable to come to her aid. They were going to work on her hair. Today. This very morning. The unreasonable panic which hit her said only one thing: run, hide. She ran, but they found her, of course. Grammy caught sight of her red blouse among the branches of her favorite pecan tree. A few well-turned threats brought her down.

Within a few mintues she was stretched out on the kitchen cabinet, her head dangling over the sink, a five-year-old sacrifice to modern cosmetology. As the cold-hot liquid oozed over her scalp, the pungent fumes that burned her skin and eyes were ignored by the woman who worked on her. Unmindful of the anguish wrought by her rubber-gloved hands, she twisted up each curl until the scalp cried for relief, wrapped the reeking mess in a towel, and sent her victim out to play, with admonition not to budge a curler. To Jana it seemed that hours of unaccustomed stillness dragged past before the neutralizer could be poured, the end papers removed, the burned and tortured hair released.

The pattern, once begun, remained unbroken. Crisp-fried curls were produced yearly by a never-ending stream of gum-popping beauty parlor ladies. One by one they bartered naturalness for loveliness in agonizing sessions under plastic curling caps.

Enduring, but never enjoying the beauty shop ordeals or their results, she saw appointments for new hair-do's become as inevitable as the changing of the seasons. From the first, Uncle Will never mentioned the new curls, and he continued to call her his little Theme Song. Nonetheless, since he often praised Vanessa's beautiful ringlets, she assumed that even he believed such tortures a necessity of life for those unfortunate enough to be born without curls.

In her twelfth summer, the magic one when Uncle Will was to spend an entire month with them, she began in mid-May to give unaccustomed attention to her appearance. A week before his arrival, to the astonishment of her mother and aunts, she actually asked permission to get her hair curled. That permission granted, she timed her appointment for the very morning his train was due in from Memphis. Somehow the agonies seemed less pronounced than usual, the odor less offensive, the wait less intolerable.

At high noon, her forehead still splotched from the chemicals she'd endured for his pleasure, she joined a small coterie of carefully groomed, heavily perspiring females who sat fanning themselves on the curved-backed golden oak benches at the depot, waiting for Uncle Will's train. Almost at once, the ladies noticed her hair.

"Oh, Jana Lee, your new hair-do is **ever** so lovely," smiled her mother's petite younger sister, Aunt Elise, mother of beautiful, spiteful Vanessa the Terrible.

"Who **did** you find to do such a good job?" purred Cousin Cornelia, the family's undisputed fashion authority whose own auburn tresses were rumored to be secretly dyed in private rituals more daring and painful than even those required for home permanents. "Why it's so **natural** looking that I thought for a moment..."

"Natural?" came the incredulous voice of ten-year-old Vanessa. "Why, I think it's **awfully** kinky. Besides," placing a hand on her hip and giving a shake of her own naturally curly raven locks, "it's **still** just dishwater blond."

Since the train's whistle brought an end to the conversation and sent everyone scurrying to the platform, Jana's stunned expression went unobserved. No one realized she hadn't followed the crowd until Uncle Will, having dutifully kissed every available cheek, looked about him in disbelief and asked, "Where's my Theme Song?"

By then, she was already halfway home. Blinded by tears she didn't understand yet couldn't stop, she had run down dusty streets, along the sun-baked highway, and through Haley's pasture. Exhausted and confused, she had slipped under the barbed wire fence that marked their field, stumbled through fresh-tassled cornstalks whose leaves slashed her bare arms and legs, and entered at last the welcome shade of the pecan orchard. With her last bit of energy, she pulled herself up into the protective branches of her favorite tree and collapsed against the rough bark of its trunk.

She came down later, of course, and when pressed for an explanation, announced to the grownups that she'd left the station to return an overdue library book. After all, there were some things more pressing than meeting the trains of distant relatives.

Uncle Will, from the impressive distance of a great-uncle, rumpled her kinky, dishwater blond head and demanded to know, "Since when must I be forsaken for library books?"

He forgave her, of course, without ever being aware of the shame she'd endured in her vain efforts to shed at long last the pet name he had given to her. They'd far more important events to discuss than her beauty parlor appointments. He wanted to see the cocoon she'd taken from the catalpa tree in midwinter. He marveled with her at the delicate house-of-becoming the creature had made and listened with interest as she explained how carefully she had broken off the twig to which it was attached by a slender, silken strand.

"You know, Theme Song," he began, looking at her through the glass jar with its network of leaves and cocoon silk, "Little girls are sort of like caterpillars. They start out kind of creepy and end up as lovely young ladies."

Caught off guard by this unexpected turn in the conversation, Jana felt her face turn a blotchy, unbecoming red. "Yes," she said without looking up, "Some do, I guess."

"They all do, honey—even Theme Songs," the grey-haired man teased. "Why, I've been working the Panama Limited for over thirty years, been a conductor for twenty, you know. That's a lot of time to watch little girls turn into butterflies. Two sisters I remember seeing go south to New Orleans every summer since they were in diapers were on the train this week. Pretty as a picture they were, too, dressed out like **McCall's** models. Yes sir, two butterflies. Wouldn't have guessed it about them a few years back. Just kids they were then, but not anymore."

Increasingly uncomfortable with this topic, Jana tried to draw him back to the fragile grey-brown cocoon in the mayonnaise jar he still held at arm's length. "Could be this one's just a moth, anyhow," she said carelessly. "Not a butterfly at all."

"You could be right," came his answer. "Maybe one of your library books will give us a clue. It won't matter, though. Moths are beautiful, too, in their own special way. Ever see a mint-green Luna moth? A big Cecropia? Or a Cynthia? They have a dusky sort of beauty, not so lacy as a butterfly."

But in the flurry of activity that always accompanied Uncle Will's visits, library research was never undertaken and the mystery of the cocoon remained unsolved. After all, there were long rides along the creek to be enjoyed on Jasmine and Nick, soft, fuzzy baby chicks to be held and admired, and an aging, foundered mare to be cared for. That was the summer Uncle Will guessed where her love of such things could be leading.

One late June afternoon as he watched her gently handling one of Hollyhock's badly deformed hooves, he said matter-of-factly, "Theme Song, you'd make a top-notch vet, you know."

Her heart seemed to stop as she knelt there on the dirt floor of the barn. "But who ever heard of lady vets?" she asked without looking up.

"So what if you're the first one in Mississippi?" he asked, unperturbed by her question. "I know there's one in West Memphis. A darn good one, too. A young lady as smart as you are and as good with animals would make a damn good horse doctor."

Though the subject never came up again on that visit or any other, Jana's mind immediately hurried her through vet school and into practice so that future visits to tend Hollyhock were made in her secret role. And even if he suspected the truth of her let's-pretend missions, Uncle Will never was so unkind as to say so. As always, he left her the freedom for dreaming and never bombarded her fantasy world with unwanted realities.

Too soon the time came for his leaving. On the evening before departure, his suitcase already packed and strapped tight, Uncle Will slowly rocked in the cane-bottomed chair on Grammy's west veranda, sipping the bourbon and water the ladies chose to ignore and taking in the rundown barn, bitterweed-invaded pasture, and straggly, unproductive hens.

As if following his glance, Grammy spoke apologetically, "Will, I know what you must be thinking, but ever since Jana's daddy left, the place has just run down. Lord knows, Lucas never did much as a farmer, but at least he could mend fence and patch barn roof. We can't afford a hired hand to do those things now. At least since Jana's got big enough and taken to tending the livestock we're doing some better. Mind you, I don't like it none, but I guess it's not going to kill her. Still, it just isn't right for a girl to be doing such rough kinds of things."

"Theme Song does all right with the chores. She does fine by the animals, too," came the soft reply. "Let her be, Sis. She's at home with the things on this farm. Let Vanessa be your Southern Lady. She's vain enough for the part. Jana's got more on her mind than soft hands and petticoats. I really believe that child . . ."

"Uncle Will, Uncle Will, come and see!" Jana's cry cut the thick summer twilight and ended adult conversation. "It's out and it's ever so strange."

Rounding the corner from the south veranda, Jana collided with her Uncle, almost dropping the jar she rammed into his chest.

In the growing darkness, the two peered through the glass. "It's a Cynthia moth you've been keeping," and with that Uncle Will flipped on the porch light and held the jar up to its glare. The moth, still wet from its borning, seemed to quicken to be near the light.

"Here, let's let it out on the front door screen. It's got to be out in the air to get dry."

Carefully, slowly, she followed his words of instruction, letting the broad-winged moth inch its way through the mouth of the jar toward the light, touching at last the mesh of the screen, a suitable place for its mooring.

"Will," came Grammy's worried voice, "what on earth's gone wrong? Is that girl all right?"

"Sure, Sis," he called back to her. "Don't try to come out here in the dark. I'll help you inside right this minute." And he slipped back around to guide her in by the west door.

Intently watching for the slightest flutter from her moth, Jana was startled as the dusky brown wings seemed to glow, their delicate purple markings taking on the richness of stained glass. The magic was Uncle Will's. He had come through the house from the side door and switched on the living room lamp. "See, Jana," he said softly, "I told you that moths can be beautiful, too."

She looked up through the screen at him, realizing he had used her real name for the first time that she could remember.

"They're more than beautiful," he continued. "They endure. They offer pleasant surprises. They don't try to be butterflies."

"Jana, Will, what's all this nonsense?" Her mother's cross voice drew nearer. "Poor Mama was chilled to the bone out there on the side porch and said you'd run off to see some butterfly."

"A moth, just a moth, Nettie dear," soothed Uncle Will, sending a wink down to Jana while putting his arm around her mother's frail shoulders. "Don't scold us. Theme Song and I just wanted to look at this moth drying its wings on the screen."

That summer had been their best one. Thereafter, when Grammy was ill, there hadn't been time for their ramblings. Her death meant an end to the farm, and once it was sold Uncle Will came only for overnight visits and those all too far in between. In fact, thinking back, she realized it had been two years since she saw him last—the summer he came home for her graduation. The day after, as they'd stood on the platform waiting for his approaching train, he had finally asked the question they'd both avoided until the last possible minute.

"Have you decided where you're going to school?"

She'd balked, knowing he remembered full well the conversation they'd had in Hollyhock's stall six years back, remembered but wasn't about to be first to discuss it. "I don't know," she began. "Mama says that Blue Mountain would put a 'fine finish' on me. She says Grammy always intended I should go there and since it's her money we'll be using . . ."

"Damn it, Theme Song!" his voice thundered in rage she had often beheld but had never had turned in her direction. "That Grammy of yours had no idea you carried a brain under that mop of hair! Let Vanessa go to Blue Mountain. That place turns out fine missionaries, librarians and housewives. But that's not what you want to be!"

He hesitated a moment, then looked into her eyes, half afraid of what he might see there. "Or is it? You tell me."

But she couldn't, for as the train rumbled in for its whistle stop, he grabbed the brass rail and, in a familiar gesture that few younger men could equal, swung smoothly aboard without even waiting for the porter to lower the steps. He hadn't waited for her answer and she'd never written to give it to him. Too late for her letter now.

"Your Uncle Will died today." She stared into the mirror, hating the spring-tight halo that met her gaze.

"Theme Song, come give your Uncle Will a kiss." She picked up the scissors and touched a drooping curl.

"It's **still** just dishwater blond." She snipped and watched the brown curl fall away.

"I've made an appointment for you next week. You're too long in the back. The curls won't hold." More cuts. "The curls won't hold."

"Don't wiggle so. You'll get this in your eyes and then you'll **really** cry." Dry-eyed, she looked with strange detachment at the shaggy contours left by scissors that refused to stop.

"You need more lift on top. A tighter wave. . . ." She ran her fingers through the stubble that remained.

"They endure. They offer pleasant surprises. They don't try to be butterflies." She let the scissors drop and spoke with softness to the close-cropped stranger in the glass. "Theme Song"—tears rose in eyes that met her own—"go tell your Uncle Will goodbye."

photo by Barbara Adams

Part III: **Caring**

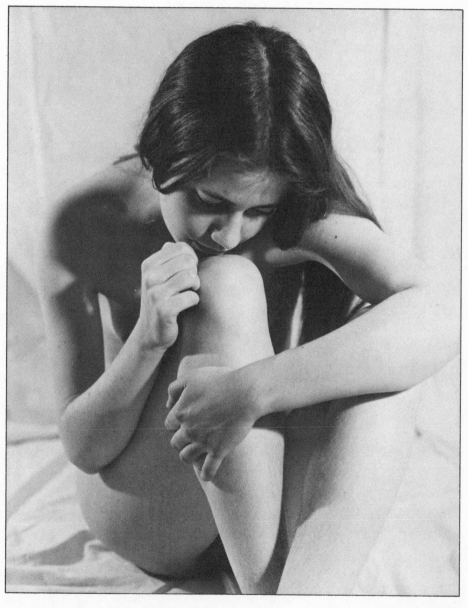

JUDITH HALL
by Emily Kay

THE FIRST COMING: BEFORE JOHN

clear sauterne and golden
sherry, canteloupe and cottage cheese,
I am ready.

under my arms & legs & thighs
I shave the curves to look hairless—
not shaved, the shell of an eaten clam, licked.

last night I rubbed in almond cream
lotion all over, even the heel rinds,
to replace natural oils that fell

into the bath water and the towel.
soaking more than 10 minutes prepares
the skin to be plucked without much

pain. take off the wiry hairs
that grow around each tit. then check
underneath for silver ones that hide.

be sure the white drop comes
out with the hair, for that is the root.
and watch other areas:

sometimes these hairs gather below
the navel or between the thighs.
I look for them almost every other week.

and when it is the afternoon before
the evening he will come, allow 2 hours
for food to move so that if he

touches skin, not a sound
will interfere. let no
canteloupe & cheese, no gas spray sauterne

and golden sherry in his presence.

Judith Hall

THE THREE BEARS

Ruth Babcock

Lavinia was the eldest, forty-six, an earthy, slightly stout woman with thick dark hair. Margaret was forty-four, taller, thinner, with a pleasant face and hair not so dark or so thick. Judith was the baby, only thirty-eight, the tallest and thinnest. She had short blond hair. Lavinia and Margaret had husbands and children. Judith was a lesbian. She had always been frank about it with her sisters, who accepted it fairly well once they got used to the idea.

The three of them were alone together for the first time in many years and they were deep in a discussion of things both inconsequential and consequential.

"Vin," said Margaret, "you have as much hair as ever, and not a single gray one. Look at all the gray in mine. I really envy you that mop."

"Huh," said Lavinia, "I'd rather have less hair on top if it would mean less all over."

"Oh, that," said Margaret. "All three of us are stuck with that."

"And all because dear old Pa was a grizzly bear," said Judith. "He should have had three sons instead of three daughters. He'd have been the first to agree, of course—not that he ever saw us nude."

"Rampant pubic hair from hip to hip," said Margaret with a sigh.

"A bushy line up the stomach to the navel," said Lavinia sadly.

"Hair on the chest," said Judith, "and fur on the legs. It's all Pop's fault. I remember when we were kids and the whole family would go to the beach on Saturdays. When Pop was in a bathing suit people would turn around and look at him."

"And giggle," said Margaret. "He looked like a rug."

"Two-inch hair all over his shoulders and back," said Lavinia.

"Say!" said Judith suddenly, "how did your husbands react to this?"

Livinia lit a cigarette. "Before I was married I was using a safety razor, and I was always terribly clumsy with it. I mean, what other bride can you think of who went to her wedding with a cut on her chin from shaving? Then after we were married that creep Daniel was always making remarks about my five o'clock shadow. The nerve! His chin was purple—even after he shaved. Mine wasn't anything like that. Then he gave me an electric razor for Christmas and it got positively cozy after that—standing in the bathroom and shaving together."

Margaret and Judith laughed, and then Margaret blushed slightly.

"When Rex and I were going together," she said, "we didn't neck very much at first—but I knew that sooner or later he'd stick his hand inside my bra and I really dreaded it."

"Well?" said Lavinia, "And did he?"

"Of course," said Margaret. "I couldn't see his face but he gave several hairs a little tug and said, 'Shall I tease you?' I said, 'No!' and he didn't—at least not until we were married." She sighed and made a wry face. "The worst of it was, he didn't have a single hair on his chest."

"I suppose being hirsute hasn't cramped your style any, Judy?" said Lavinia.

"Not in the long run, no. But Migg's story reminds me of something that happened very early on. I was only seventeen."

Lavinia and Margaret leaned forward expectantly. They enjoyed hearing accounts of Judith's experiences, particularly since they were always shocked by them.

"When I was a freshman in college I fell madly in love with another girl in the dorm, and it was quite mutual. That was Bev; you might remember her name."

Both sisters looked blank.

"Bev and I were so close that her parents got worried because she wasn't going out with boys, and in the middle of a semester they took her out of school and sent her to a college back east. For the last three nights before she left I went to her room and got in bed with her for a while. We had to be awfully careful because the rules were strict and the house mother was always snooping around."

"I remember that nosy old bag," said Lavinia. "She caught me climbing in the window one night. Well, I suppose you two really lived it up."

"On the contrary," said Judith, "we were seventeen, totally unsophisticated and inexperienced. We'd been in bed together before but except for general embracing we'd never touched each other below the neck. Oh, maybe around the waist, but never between the neck and the waist, and anything below the waist was unthinkable."

"Well, what was allowed?" said Margaret.

"Lots and lots of hugging and kissing. It goes without saying we never took any clothes off. We were very tender. The whole thing seemed sort of sacred to us, even when our insides were churning. We looked at each other a lot and uttered many words of love.

"Well, now that Bev was going away, we were in absolute despair. The first of those last three nights we lay in each other's arms, crying and kissing and declaring that we would die without each other."

"Ah, youth," murmured Lavinia.

Judith smiled. "The second night was different. I slid in on Bev's right side again and we clung to each other. But after some kisses and tears we lay on our backs, sort of facing each other and stroking each other's hair and cheeks. Then, breathlessly, we began to stroke shoulders and arms, and almost simultaneously we each laid a hand very gently on a breast—my left and her right."

"Do you have to be so specific?" said Margaret.

"Yes. You'll see. Once we got there we were practically paralyzed. We couldn't breathe or move or speak.

"Finally after a while I raised up on one elbow, leaned over and very lightly kissed her right breast—through her pajamas, of course. They I lay down and she just as lightly kissed my left breast, also through my pajamas. Then in a complete daze I got up and went back to my room."

"But you had one more night," said Margaret.

"Right. And just before I went to Bev's room the third night I very carefully shaved all the hairs off my left breast."

Lavinia snorted, "Oh, come on Judy—"

"Yes, I did," said Judith. "The left one. And that night we got to where we'd left off the night before, and after a while I delicately, oh so delicately lifted her pajama top and kissed her right breast very lightly. And then she delicately lifted my pajama top and kissed my left breast. Then we covered up and lay on our backs all speechless and quivering. We felt that our love had been completely consummated. When we could speak again we whispered that we would belong to each other forever. Then we clung together and cried, and I went back to my room."

"Honestly, Judy," said Margaret, "do you expect us to believe that you shaved only one side?"

"So help me, that's exactly what I did."

"But how could you be so sure she wouldn't touch the other one?"

"I don't know. I've never been that sure of anything since, but I knew positively that she wouldn't."

"Well, what if she had? How would you have felt?" asked Margaret.

"I'd have died of embarrassment. At that time in my life I felt like a freak."

"Then I just can't believe you would take such a chance," Margaret said. "It would have been so easy to shave them both."

"Why bother?" said Judith, "when I knew what was going to happen?" She laughed and stood up. "I have to leave," she said. "I have a date with someone who loves every hair." She kissed her sisters and went to the door.

"By the way," she said just before she went out, "her name's Bev."

DAY OF SEX

We let day break at noon,
when the light first stirred us
awake in the roughest way.
We knocked our heads together and
mud rose in our veins.

Outside the clouds bared
their blue secrets.
It rained hair for hours.

                    Elizabeth Goldman

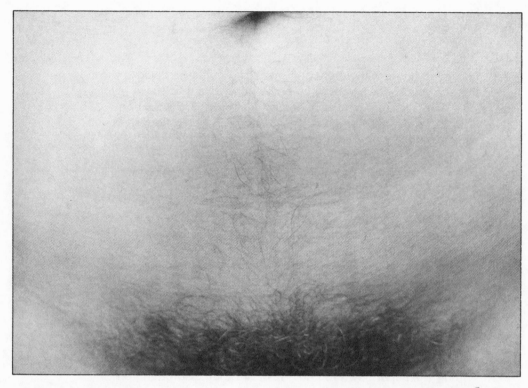

photo by Laurie Bronstein

BATH

Oiled by fragrant waters
wispy seaweed patch
moves with subtle currents
caused by hands that tease
hovering and covering
dark, inviting boundaries
floating, tangled thatch.

Linda Sellers Peavy

from THE FIFTH DAY OF JANUARY

I have left home without shaving my legs. I could go back,
there is time. I don't want to go back. I don't want to shave my
legs. A month ago I let my underarm hair grow. I checked on
it daily in the bathroom glass, speculating if it would flourish or
hang in skinny wisps like my pubic hair when it grew back
after being shaved. Then I shaved, I shaved my legs too.
Because I was going to the doctor. Because I was afraid my
hair would repulse him.

When Maude changed her jeans in Linda's living room her
pubic hair was thick as the hills after spring rains. I want to fall
into the hills, be lost to everything. I began to see Maude not
as an older woman but voluptuous, capable of orgiastic sex.
Maude's husband is a doctor. A man on my street speaks of
the pubic hairs of black women who have been murdered, how
long they are. He has invented a machine to study body
specimens of victims of crime.

I am in my doctor's dressing room and he is through with me.
I rip off the paper gown to find a rash of mouths sprouting on
my chest and throat, like the radishes my mother cut in
rosettes for her parties. My underarms are hairless.

Phyllis Koestenbaum

Mother, I'm letting it grow,
enjoying letting it grow—
the thick brown hairs
on my thighs
you made me shave
for beaches and parades.

I'm letting it grow, Ma,
dark and curling as creeping ivy
to see if there's a man alive
who'll have the guts
to walk with me in shorts
down streets, in public places.

And if there's not—
I'll die it black
and grow it thick and wilder;
naked hair will trail
like banners through the crowds—
all eyes glued to these gorilla legs
as they plod forth like Kong,
hairy and alone
but in their own direction.

Nancy Blotter

MY HAIR

For almost a year I let it grow
dark and sassy down the legs
my mother always praised
because (she said) hers were like a chicken's.

Women are not supposed to seem to have it,
so in private defiance
I stopped shaving in mid-July
after teaching the summer course,
when there were few people who would see me.
It took getting used to.

My husband liked it.
We went away to Maine
and when I wore my bathing suit
I watched the new growth
cling to my ankles in water
and dry like young seaweed in the sun.
In the fall and winter
it didn't show beneath dark stockings and pants,
but in bed I liked to touch it,
soft and long beneath my fingers.

When I visited my mother
she said it was disgusting.

Spring came with warm winds
that riffled through it
the day I first wore shorts.
I looked forward to the sun
that would make it gleam brighter.
But then something changed

inside me, I don't know what, perhaps
forsythia drained my will,
perhaps dandelions made me stronger,
I shrank or grew, I
still do not understand;

but suddenly today
I shaved it off,
the electric razor making smooth clean swipes
down the pale lengths of my legs.
What I'd grown for almost a year
was gone in five minutes,
my skin licked naked
by metal tongues encased in pink plastic.

My husband stroked my calf,
said it was different, all right.
He does not understand either, doesn't ask.
Now the wind wanders by me
hardly noticed;
I have begun to toughen again.

My mother will be pleased.

Katharyn Machan Aal

HAIR

1.

I have grown accustomed
to the hair on my legs
and even wear them bare
in public.

I have a certain fondness
for the dark silk strands
under my arms
they don't prickle or sting.
When I was twelve one day
my mother expelled a gasp
told me to lower my arms
she didn't want to see the sprouts
which told that we were both
growing old.
Peeking under
I kept daily count
for months.

My fingers warmly twirl
the long wiry tendrils
which slope a trail to my navel.
A lover once thought
they were sexy.

I love the hair on my head
deep auburn, baby fine
I grow it long, shiny to my thigh
and wear it down
for special occasions.

It is the hair on the center
of my senses
I could not learn
to call my own.

2.

The face I could not hide
I tried
peroxide and gentle explanations:
everyone has hair there, mine
is just darker. But
I could not believe eyes
targeted to my smile.

For years a child hears
whispers: she
has a mustache
her mother has a beard.
She wouldn't be seen
with her mother
paid guilt for the shame
she wanted them both to be pretty.

3.

Pin prick sacrifices
to that young girl
I bear electrocution
root by root
and pay dearly.

You would be surprised
she said,
really amazed at the number
of women who have
this done.

She is wrong.
I find no surprise
nor in other things women hide from
each other, from their own
sex.

I ask her to leave
the long fine hairs growing
along my chin.
I will be the only one who knows.

Edith Walden

MY MOTHER'S MOUSTACHE

My mother said I'd inherit a moustache and I did.
Hers she removed with green wax she melted in a pan,
   a two-inch saucepan,
      when the hairs grew too evident.
At fifteen, a dutiful daughter and fascinated
as well by my possible beauty, I bought my own
   doll-size waxworks and inherited
      my mother's ritual for a while.
I'd cook my wax, let it cool a little before spreading
it on; then I would wait for the unnatural stuff
   (this wasn't at all
      like candlewax; it never flaked)
to harden, and eyes shut, I'd rip it all off in one piece,
relishing the hot pain, the gasping pores—ignoring
   the tears my eyes spewed against my will,
      the cowards! The first time was the worst.
My peach-fuzz moustache which I thought too bushy for beauty
was blonde and soft; wax would not guarantee new face-hair
   as blonde or as soft.
      Even my mother said "After
the first waxing a moustache becomes darker and thicker."
But, defying heredity and believing in
   perfectibility, I began,
      new bare-faced hopes throbbing through the pain.
It was hairless for a time. I waited, climbed on the sink
to get nearer the mirror. "Let nothing grow!" No luck.
   Sprouts pushed through my skin.
      I'd read of Russian princesses
whose lovers saw their moustaches as signs of great beauty;
now I imagined singing mezzo at La Scala,
   moustache flowing to Puccini, like
      the dark diva who smiles with Bjoerling
(Angel's long-playing **La Boheme.**) I stroked my new dark
hairs, vowed to keep them, and did until pink powder turned
   my moustache orange.
      I returned to the ritual,
waxing once a month and it took me six years to rebel.
I switched to cream, a less utilitarian means.
   The results were disastrous: It smelled
      destructive, demanded more treatments,
caused pink eruptions near my mouth, uglier than the hair.
I tried a second brand, two creams: one opaque, scented
   rose for removal,
      the other clear, an after-cream

to soothe the skin, prevent pimples. It did not work at all.
I had tampered with the nature of my face. I yearned
   to be fresh-faced, windblown, organic
      or even hairy. I let it grow.
My inheritance re-emerged black and stiffer. I
struggled to find it beautiful for myself and my heirs,
   ignored my penchant
      to see my image as bristling,
rejoiced secretly when the summer sun turned me blonder
and my moustache invisible, and hoped for a flash,
   a permanent paling, an end to
      bouts with demons whose hairy fingers
would never quit my face and allow even two inches
of blonde lip. October came and diluted my tan.
   In November my
      blonde hairs vanished. December brought
back the brunette. I wanted peace and no hair. I settled
for compromise. I perform new rites of whitening:
   On a minute white tray, I blend one
      part "accelerating" powder with
two parts "greaseless" white cream, making sure that I am thorough.
Then, carefully, with a tiny white spoon (both these tools
   come in the bleach box),
      I spread the paste around my lips,
let it dry twelve minutes (no cooking, no pain, no mess) while
it surreptitiously softens and whitens, lightens
   even brightens the surfacing
      memory, my mother's moustache.

Honor Moore

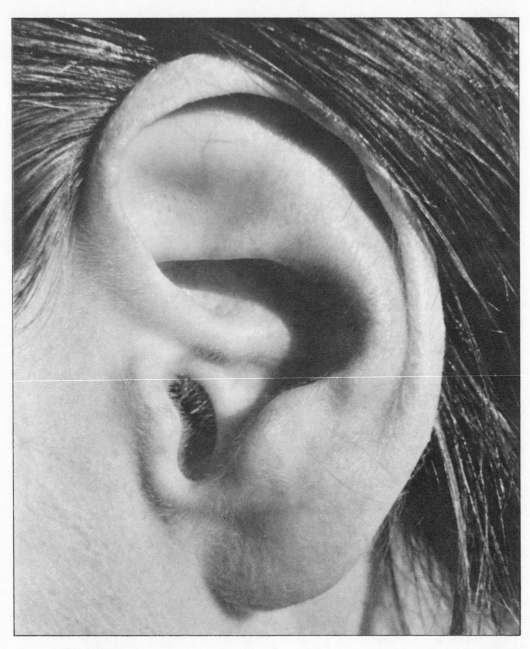

EAR HAIR
by Kathy Morris and Marc Weiss

HAIR TODAY, DOWN TOMORROW

Zane Kotker

Hermaphrodite   It is in my nature to keep my eyes open for atavistic sights and remnants of myth and I do so on upper Broadway, U.S.A., where I do most of my walking, so it was not unusual that I should be the one in the shoe store to see the Hermaphrodite. I went in to pick up a pair of sneakers for my son and was waiting at the counter when my eye was held by a customer's leg on which was a mass of black hairs. What is a grown man doing buying shoes in a children's shoe store? I raised my eyes above the rolled up dungarees to the torso and face of a young woman. Back to the hairy leg, up to the face, etc. This is my first hermaphrodite, part of my brain remarked to another, as I paid my twelve dollars for Keds and got out.

On Broadway were the real hermaphrodites, black men in elegant drag and well-groomed women whose sex-change operations had rendered their initial maleness almost undetectable—though every nearby eye was busily detecting. Why should I be staggered by a little hair on a slender female leg? Actually, it was a lot of hair. I have slender legs. "She must be one of those feminists," a synaptic spokesman of mine proposed. "One of **those** feminists?" A countering reprimand. It is remarkable how easily I can separate myself from the political movement that means most to me and with which I am most identified. Yet I do it when most feminists do it, when my own femininity is attacked: this, of course, is the most powerful weapon of the adversaries of the movement—the nuclear bomb of sexual politics, to which immunities develop slowly, if at all. But why should my femininity be so attacked by leg hair?

Why is leg hair considered more male than female if both of us have it?

Rad-lib   In the sixties a few folks predicted that hairy female legs would be the rule by the mid-seventies. Women would refuse to shave the hair off their legs in a movement toward androgyny and, perhaps, as a swing of novelty. Women weren't any longer going to shave to please men; it was too much of a bother and their bodies were their own now.

A blond shaver with the high forehead of a Roger Van der Weyden madonna told me recently that this phenomenon was on the wane. "Yes, you know, it was a Rad-Lib thing to do. None of us were shaving in '73, '74, '75. It was after the war, you know, it was a protest. What else could we do? But only one or two of us aren't shaving now." A roomful of twenty-year-olds with hairy legs stuck into their bunny slippers came to mind, but perhaps they don't wear bunny slippers anymore either. "And the two who still don't shave?" "Oh, I guess they were just more radical, or stronger feminists, or maybe their men liked hair." She was whisked away and made unavailable for further interviewing.

She's wrong, though; my daily rides on a bus assure me that the unshaven look is not fading with lost wars or acquired B. A.'s. Why women aren't shaving is less clear. Most say, "It's a bother" or "I like a natural look." But why didn't they say that in 1950?

Hairy Men   Hairy men: I adore them! Hair curling up over their shirt buttons, hair running down the back of their necks, hair when they roll up their sleeves, hair on their legs when they come dripping out of the ocean. My favorite husband in children's literature was Jo March's Professor Bhaer. I remember nothing about him now except that he was hairy and bearded and, by implication, older, wiser, and infinitely more attractive than little Amy's beardless Laurie, the boy next door. This may be entirely inaccurate, what I have remembered; it may stem only from the name Professor Bhaer which I had initially remembered as Papa Bear.

My favorite lovers were Robin Hood, the Lone Ranger, and Tarzan; since the first two never took off the rather long underwear that served them for clothes, I'm faced first with Tarzan, the Apeman. My darling! We used to have long talks in the woods, Tarzan and I, though I believe we eschewed latinate words and stuck to simple English. My head came about to his hairy chest and when he picked me up in his arms for a swing through the vines, I believe I became suddenly rather a lot smaller. Oh Daddy! I recall that he was careful to teach me to swing on my own vine and to recognize when I could do so unaided. Robin Hood was probably not so hairy since he was given to deeper conversation in the woods—on inequality, with occasional asides about my beauty. As for the Lone Ranger, he just rode on and on, out of the woods and onto the plains, and he always made me sit on the back of the horse. I was growing older.

My father was not what we called in Sunday School "an hairy man," yet hairiness is "father" to me, as well as "male."

History   There was a time when early tropical man shaved himself free of his body hair. Dodingo brides of the Uganda area spent the two weeks before marriage having their pubic hair plucked by their mothers, mothers who must have appeared before eyes hazy from heat and pain as the evilest of stepmothers. Their heads were shaved, too, and every bit of fuzz rubbed off their bodies. The ancient Egyptians did the same thing, and not just the brides. Aristocratic men and women got rid of all their body hair, including that on their heads: the beards of the pharoahs were wigs. Shaving, or using plaster and pumice, was a necessity for good hygiene. And in a culture that valued formal and beautifully crafted objects, the naked body was itself to be cultivated and transformed—dead or alive. (Would there be hair on a Brett Weston nude?) The women of ancient Greece shaved and Greek boys shaved their legs, as their contribution to the homosexual society which saw them as junior or female partners. When they were fully grown, they didn't shave their legs anymore, but I am this minute looking at a reproduction of Hercules from a fourth century B.C. vase and he hasn't got any pubic hair. Roman women shaved themselves, too. At some unknown date after the hairy Hun, they were still plucking pubic hair into shape, but total depilation was ceasing to be common. When the Holy Roman Empire's crusading knights came home from the Near East, they brought back with them the secret of the harems: shaven women. Again, the ladies of the western courts and aristocracies took to pulling out pubic hair or ripping it off with plasters. Catherine de Medici put a stop to it: it hurts too much, she said. Such depilation became a treatment for hysteria; the blood rushed to the pulled roots and left the "heated" head.

Our American grandmothers most likely did not shave beneath their Victorian blouses or skirts. But our mothers were probably shaving from after the First World War, though their fathers insisted it was unlady like. You can imagine who shaves! Not my daughter! It was either masculine or whorish, the parents said. But perfectly innocent high schoolers went on shaving away the fluff below the knee and under the arm. Their fathers relented and advised them to use some soap and water with the razor. The girls dried their legs, put on their sand-colored "Sahara" stock-ings, and draped themselves in short mummy-sheath dresses patterned after the Egyptian costumes revealed in the great ex-cavation of Tutankhamen's tomb.

We had our mothers to tell us how to shave; some of us will not be passing this knowledge on to our daughters.

Five Areas   "There are five hairless parts of the body," I propound at supper. "The lips, the palms, the soles, the nipples, and parts of the genitalia."

"You forgot the fingernails," my daughter says.

"And the eyeballs," my son says.

They didn't ask me what genitalia means.

"Those five parts are the most sensitive to the touch," I say. They laugh.

I try it again at somebody else's dinner table. The guests are hostile; the host shows me how there isn't any hair on his fingers between the knuckles and the fingertips. But then everybody has something to say about wax jobs, the sugar treatments in Israel, Park Avenue dermotologists, male homosexuals who shave their legs, or the guileless, hairy Esau. They like to talk about other people's hair.

Race/Class   We have as many hairs on our bodies as does your average chimpanzee; ours is just shorter and lighter. We may have lost longer hair after we left Eden and its trees to run around in the hot sun on the open plains after prey. We didn't have a chance hunting at night when the faster cats and dogs were out doing it; we had to take daytime. It helped keep cool to sweat and you sweat better where you don't have hair. That is, less hair means more sweat glands and faster cooling. But you need hair on top of your head to keep your brains from boiling over. A man with long legs, a thick Afro and relatively little hair on arms and chest must be from a gene pool that favored such running and such a cooling system. The men in my gene pool must have spent a long time in the cooler latitudes of the Angles, the Saxons, and the Celts. I don't have nothing to do with them Jutes. Body hair is ethnic.

In Mexico, I'm told, women of Spanish descent don't shave under their arms, in order to proclaim their lack of Indian blood. Indians are even less hairy than blacks, being of Mongol gene pools; the Mongols are the least hairy of men. This is reminiscent of Roman days: when the upper class shaved, the slaves had to cultivate beards. When harelip or a wrinkled neck caused an emperor to grow a covering beard, his nobles and their brothers and their uncles grew beards; but his slaves had to shave theirs off.

The First Shave   I began to shave my legs and underarms when I was a sophomore in high school and I did it in the one bathroom of my family's house. In that bathroom was a tub with a hose you could twist into a shower, the usual toilet, a window which opened onto the vista of a backyard in Hartford, Connecticut, a sink, and a medicine cabinet in which I kept my razor. "You musn't shave with anybody else's razor, you'll get infected." One Christmas before, my brother had given me a copy of THE DIARY OF ANNE FRANK. For reasons I have now forgotten, I read it in that bathroom, sitting on the rug where I sometimes slept if taken with the terrors by night. It was pink, as I recall, pale bathroom pink. Here I sat reading Anne Frank in a blush of pride: my brother considered me capable of reading a real book and a girl my own age had written down thoughts that grown-ups valued enough to print. Neither point had been made to me before. Indeed, in the back of the ANNE FRANK was some kind of analytical writing which called into question whether such a young girl could actually have written those thoughts. It dealt with the validity of a rumor that perhaps her father had produced the diary in memory of her. Luckily, I did not read this first, because all the way through the early section—before Anne was exposed to things I have not had to meet—I kept thinking, "She's just like me! She thinks the same thoughts I do!" The world was a lucid combination of the real and surreal to me that year; thirteen, I believe, is the peak of intellectuality. The veil of puberty dropped before those clear eyes shortly thereafter and I began to shave my legs standing on that pink rug.

You start with the left because you can balance better standing on your right foot. You soap up the leg with warm water; the first time, you ask yourself, Hot? Cold? Not too much soap, not a foam. You run the razor under the water faucet. By now the tendon in the inner thigh is a bit pulled, but not bad. You start at the ankle and work up. Past the anklebone where you have to be very careful not to nick. Along the shinbone you must angle carefully, too; for slender legs it's good to keep the tendon flexed so the bone is not a ridge. Up past the scar where I crawled on a piece of broken glass by the lilac bushes at a game of hide-and-seek on my fourth Fourth of July in another backyard on top of a mountain in Vermont. "Cheat!" My brother called as I limped, bleeding, for the house. "You can't quit playing just because of that!" The little indentations of the knee are treacherous. From here, if not from the ankle or the shinbone, the sudden spouts of blood will appear. There it is! Always so surprisingly red! She lives! Not bad, a little piece of toilet paper torn off and placed over the bleeding will do fine. A relief to lower that leg; the tendon shakes and is quiet. Now the right leg, wobbling on the left foot. This leg had then no scars to mark the past. It does now: a white place behind the tendon of the ankle—plenty of bleeding there from shaving and on the same day during freshman year at college that I had been contemplating freshman-year suicide. On the kneecap: another white line whose origin I have forgotten because it arrived after childhood and is not important, not part of my real body. But the girl back there in the bathroom hasn't gone to college yet. It is summer in Hartford, a hot town. Flies are buzzing at the bathroom screen; she is shaving her legs for the first time. Then under the arms.

She takes off her glasses because otherwise the underarm is too close. This is too near the heart! I could cut right into it! I could bleed to death! Soap and water, she said, that will make it easier. Carefully, very carefully; God wants us to live. The world is good. He is kind. Don't make a slip. The right arm seems even harder to turn the neck toward; also, the left hand is less trusted. Save this for the last job, as you save liver and squash—maybe you will not have to eat them. But no, you cannot go onto the beach at Black Point with one of the four crucial areas unprepared to meet its maker or its mate. At last she is finished; people are knocking politely on the bathroom door, it is New England. She rubs her hand along the right leg, very smooth. Ravishable. Will she be ravished at Black Point? The steam-wilted copy of ANNE FRANK is holding up the window frame; from now on, thought, as well as body hair, must be sloughed off—neither is feminine.

Into the bedroom, the red and white bathing suit, the full-length mirror. Indeed, life **will** be lived within its glassy, satisfying surface for some years. The bride is shorn; gentlemen, step up and take your pick! She is finished, she is ready, Frau Kum! German soldiers are running down a city street, cutting through doors with bayoneted rifles. The war is on. But she is very pleased; she lights a Lucky Strike and poses languidly in the mirror. In girls it goes this way: breasts, pubic hair, menstruation, and finally, hair under the arms and on the arms and legs. And then, who knows. . . .It won't be long now. She restatues her legs and takes a slow inhale.

So why aren't women shaving anymore?

Perfection   Marjorie Stoddard was my friend in first grade. In second grade she moved away from our little town in Vermont and set herself up in Springfield, a metropolis. I took the train all by myself to see her, my frist trip. We had a good time, though, of course, reunions are not life. We got into our bathing suits one day and so did Marjorie's mother; we went out the back door of their second floor apartment and stood while Marjorie's mother held open the screen door and checked things in her lunch basket. Under Marjorie's mother's arm I could see one hair, maybe two, that she had missed in shaving.

Terrible! The perfection of all future life was marred. Though I would make no such error as a woman, the thought that others could so carelessly open the door to flaws was a threat. And I did not want flaws in Marjorie's mother because I was in love with Marjorie's father, about whom I had privileged information. "I dreamt I saw my father's dong"—Vermonters had their own vocabularies even then—Marjorie had reported to me one morning in grade one of the two-room schoolhouse. "It was pink and brown." Pink and brown, the beloved object itself and the pubic hair surrounding it, no doubt glimpsed some cool October evening in the corridor outside the bathroom. I had loved her father from that day on. Pink linen dresses edged with brown braiding hanging from bars in Saks Fifth Avenue still bring Mr. Stoddard, in all his glory, to mind.

The specter of Mrs. Stoddard by the screen door no longer haunts me. I forget to shave from time to time and my silverware is seldom polished. Life did not turn out to be so orderly and controllable as I had supposed when my mother was picking up after me and ironing my blouses. If I had been lulled into thinking adulthood would be mostly white lace and black lace romances, spotted with scenes of triumph at the brain surgeon's table, on the ballet stage, and among the poet-seers of that Wilderness, New York, I learned to deal with it. Mrs. Stoddard did not spoil my future; it is still the time for me next week, next month, next year when I will be sitting gracefully on my dining chair and wearing an Indian sari, while my charming and well-combed children carry drinks on silver trays to my amusing guests; it is the very evening I have finished my novel again and I've done it all with armpits on which there is not one hair. Thank you, Mrs. Stoddard, I have, from time to time, forgiven you for your immense gaucherie, your slip into the pit that leads to death.

Naked   Before I had any, the idea of pubic hair on my own body seemed as much a flaw as Mrs. Stoddard's triumphant hairs. I sat in the bath assuming, as I now assume I will never grow older, that I would never be altered in the smoothness of my skin by such a dark and alien element. A few years ago I saw that same body in my tub. I knew you were still there! It was my daughter sitting there with her long legs stretched out in the water. I am still seven, fully formed and forever stabilized; what I see in the mirror is cellular overlay.

One night when I was actually seven, my mother sat in a chair in my bedroom in Vermont and smiled at me while I ran around the room naked except for one addition to my true and complete self: her best necklace of amber beads which were heavy and cold on my chest, though they seemed to hold the light of the sun inside them. I cavorted and posed; I sang and jumped; my mother smiled. Frequently I sit on the edge of a bed here on upper Broadway and watch an almost identical body dashing about, at once flamboyant and modest—"lock the door!" I smile, out of love: for myself? for her? for the world?

Fathers and brothers remember those bodies, too. Earlier societies may have shaved their bodies because lice aren't nice and crabs are worse, but once smoothed and shorn of hair, the depilated bride is also someone who lurks in the chemicals of the brain. A gentleman friend who had discovered a woman who shaved her pubic hair said this: "It was a shock at first, but the reason I loved it so much was that when I was about nine or ten we had a little club of kids in the neighborhood and we used to go into an unoccupied garage and take off our clothes and mostly just look at each other. We didn't have any pubic hair then, any of us, and there was one girl I especially liked . . . in Europe with this woman who shaved, I kept thinking of that girl." D. H. Lawrence and another friend of mine share a repulsion of it: my friend had tried, at ten, to approach his eight-year-old sister. Now he likes women with lots of pubic hair.

King Kong   The possibility of hair and fingernails growing so long they swell the coffin lid are among the acts of God which I con-gratulate myself on having firmly rejected. King Kong is what we have come from, not that to which we go. The other night my husband, son, daughter, and I watched the original Kong on television. Teeny tiny bloodless and hairless Fay Wray is kissed by a passionate sailor and shortly thereafter let loose onto an island where the presence of the chest-beating Kong belittles all else. In his gigantic dark hairy hand he raises her to his lips. He is the ultimate animal and she the spirit that will never die; and she tames him, don't forget. For if he hadn't been concerned about her welfare on the Empire State Building, I think he might not have been shot off it. Our lights went out, the television went off and we left the room. Our son walked stoically to his room; for the first time in his life he did not want us to linger or to say good-night. Sad-eyed and filled with sorry, he shut his own door.

We stood outside to monitor the disorder and the sorrow that we sensed: "He knows the beast within him must die," my husband said.

I went then into my daughter's room where she lay, a miniature Fay-Marilyn on her bed. "Kiss me the way he kissed Fay Wray!" She squealed and circled her arms around me to pull me down and kiss me on the lips the way we don't do at my house. She is transformed. How will she wait until she's sixteen? I open her window for the cool winds of night, thinking of girls who love to ride horses. He had to give up the animal within; she got to keep it, delivered in a docile sailor suit.

Male and Female

Foetuses are covered with a fine down they usually lose just before birth, being born boy or girl with all the hair follicles for hirsuteness, including those of mustache and beard. Estrogen in girls keeps the hair from growing in, at least until menopause, when the hormone's reduction can provide a bearded lady. Hairs on the female face or chest seem to be among the most horrifying of growths. "She took her blouse off and there it was," a friend confided to me. "Not a little bit, not downy. But real hair, all over her chest, between her breasts, just like a man's." He hadn't been able to summon up the necessary enthusiasm to conclude the night in the style to which he was accustomed. No more than could the various legendary lecherous old gents who have chased virginal maids into the corners of sacred folklore, where the maids pause, turn their backs, raise their eyes to heaven, and then pivot gracefully around to reveal a full beard. The satyrs freeze so rapidly, they can barely run off. A beard wig in the pocketbook might be more of a resource to urban women walking dark streets than the pocket police alarm or a packet of Mace.

Hair on the legs seems to come next in its ability to raise disgust. "Under the arms is okay, but if a woman lets hair grow on her legs I feel she's imitating me and is too devout a feminist for me to love." "She's imitating you?" "Yes." "But if she doesn't shave under her arms, she's not imitating you?" "Right." "But that's illogical." "I know. Maybe if she has blond hair, it's okay."

Hair under the female arm seems less troubling than on the leg. Alex Comfort even recommends it, and for the same reason that evolution initially commended it. Sweat evaporates more slowly where there is hair and underarm perspiration needs to stay in contact with the air in order to reach the peak odor that impelled primeval man to seek after primeval woman. No man I've talked to has mentioned this. Most of them say, "It's okay, I got used to it." A few take it as a token of pubic hair and think it suggests a turbulent sexuality. If the "feminine" ideal is hairless, smooth, and blond in the Fay Wray tradition, her darker sister with the thick eyebrows, the bit of hair on her forearms and under her arms is, for a number of men, more the "sexual" ideal. Interesting that the blond more approximates the child's coloring and quantity of hair covering. The shaved late Medieval Roger Van der Weyden forehead was very much a "Baby Doll" look.

Men achieve dominance by hair: the more hair, the fiercer; quite simply, you appear to occupy more space if you've got fuzz all over you, so you look bigger—like a cat whose hair is standing on end. I look up from my book at the library into the bent faces of two men who are reading: one has curly hair and one is clean shaven. Something strikes me about them, but it's unclear. My eye returns to the bushy fellow. I like him better. He's more exciting. I imagine he will look up and our eyes will meet. He looks up. I look down; I wasn't brought up in the old days for nothing. He looks down. I look up, but at the other man. Then I see what it was; their faces are remarkably similar. It was the furry hair that led me to make my choice. He is a warrior who will fuss with his hair before going into battle; I will be inventing agriculture back outside the cave. Polarity is important.

Not the smart-dumb polarity, not the adult-child polarity; and that's the problem, how to drop the sour kumquats from the old system without spoiling the grapes? But why do I see myself back at the cave? Why not out on the front lines? Is it acculturation?

Clark Gable shaved under his arms. Every day.

Sheba   I am not someone convinced that prehistoric matriarchies really existed; it seems possible to me that these hypothetical societies may be the shadows of the actual early matriarchy in all our lives: Mom. In an old gloss on the Biblical story of Solomon and Sheba, there was one city left in the world not under Solomon's domain: Kitor, in the land of Sheba, where the roots of the trees went right down to Eden and folks knew not the art of war—they didn't even have bows and arrows. They were ruled by a woman whom Solomon sent for. Rather heavily, he suggested she pay him a call of submission and when she came into his presence with gifts, she viewed him across a shiny glass floor she took to be a shallow reflecting pool. She raised her skirts to keep them out of the water and proceeded toward him. But she hadn't shaved her legs. "Your beauty is the beauty of a woman, but your hair is masculine," Solomon said to her. "Hair is an ornament to a man, but it disfigures a woman." He was seldom at a loss for words. One gets the feeling that Sheba was going to be losing the hair as well as the kingdom she was born with. Solomon had, indeed, meant the floor for a reflecting surface, since he had been told Sheba did not shave and he wanted to find out for himself. The rumor that she did not shave had been started by those who wished to malign her as a demon: both male and female demons were covered with body hair in those days, as were witches. Solomon ordered up a depilatory for Sheba and married her. In later centuries, witches were shaved all over their bodies to reveal the vows to Satan that might be seen in various marks on their skin. Androgyny is frightening—in hair as well as in the power of a queen.

Infant   I have been editing a book about Russia, in which there is a scene where a man goes to the grave of his wife who died in a prison camp. He is escorted to an aisle of trees in amongst which are the mounds of graves. The man throws himself upon the grave of the wife whom he has not seen for ten years. He clutches at the tall grass that grows over the mound of earth and whispers into the grave below. Here I have to stop. I have read the book three times, and each time I had to get up for the Kleenex. Why do I cry? Obviously, it's sad and I care about the man whispering to the skeleton below, though the woman in the book has been no more fleshed out than the "bare bones" in the grave. I think I am crying because he is clutching the grass. Perhaps that alone, or perhaps clutching the grass plus whispering. Why? Because he is as a tiny child, a newborn mammal hanging onto the furry stomach of a gigantic mama who hears him whimper and cry distantly; but who perhaps only stirs herself to waddle off, the pendulum of her swaying belly spotted with a litter of little creatures clutching at her hair. She is indifferent; she might turn and devour them any minute and cause them to be like the bare bones already within her, for she is also the earth. I think I am crying out of infant terror.

Hair is mother; hair is father; Tarzan lives in the woods. I do not believe that these are residual memories, but other people will cry at that passage too, and it won't be for the hero or his dead wife.

Anxiety   Shaving with an electric razor helps allay the anxiety of cutting your legs and bleeding, but the basic anxiety of altering the body lingers. If my heel should touch the water dripping from the faucet, will I be electrocuted? It's not the same when you file your nails; the nails are not easily broken through to the inside. We all fall under Dr. Spock's description of the child who needs the bandaid for the scraped knee because he's afraid the inside of him will spill out and he will die. To alter the body in any way is to touch upon the basic anxiety of the organism. I look up into today's mirror: I have been ravished. Will I be ravaged?

The Animal   We love the animal in ourselves; we hate plastic wrap. We prefer a rough woven Irish wool sweater to an English bone china teacup—we call it "finer work." We are the first generation to do so. We want to build houses out of old beer cans and heat them by the light of the sun: we're scared. The animal and its instincts have suddenly become the key to keep the world from blowing up or drowning in its litter. We want our hair natural and we don't pray for a wraith-like immortality anymore—blond, pre-sexual, with, maybe, wings. Mortality is just fine, thanks; after the three score wonderful and the ten so-so years. Perhaps this desire for what's "natural" is why women are not shaving their legs. Many of them say so and they report they love the silky feel of the hair that grows past stubble on their legs. It must be pretty hard to turn over in a mummy case. Our age would not be compelled to shave off a witch's body hair, because hair does not frighten us: to be an animal is to be saved. That way God still loves us and will handle air pollution.

Besides, we don't have lice.

Acculturation   Across from me on a bus are two young women. One is blond and her legs are covered with a blond fuzz. The other is brown-haired and on her legs is a dark fuzz.

The blond fuzz, I think to myself, is not so bad. The dark fuzz is repulsive. Well, I congratulate myself, I've come a long way.

118

When I first started thinking about this, I would have had an instinctive stomach-clutching response to both.

Who am I to make judgements on what they do with their body hair?

I know already what they would say if I should ask them why they don't shave: "It's a bore. I like to be natural. Why should I shave just because men like women with smooth legs? Let them shave!"

I cannot disagree with any of those reasons. Why doesn't it look repulsive to them?

Why does it look repulsive to me?

Something has happened in their eyes that has not happened in mine.

They have shed a layer of culture—not chronological, not backwards in time to "animal," but out of the culture they were raised in. As Copernicus saw the world without its accustomed veil. How did they do that?

Suddenly I love them both. But their legs look repulsive. I am old.

Notes on Contributors

KATHARYN MACHAN AAL, editor of RAPUNZEL, RAPUNZEL, teaches in the Applied Writing Program of Ithaca College and is Coordinator of the Ithaca Community Poets. Her poetry and fiction have appeared in numerous little magazines, and in 1977 Gehry Press published her collection of poems entitled THE BOOK OF THE RACCOON. She is a member of the Feminist Writers' Guild. Again she has stopped shaving.

BARBARA ADAMS teaches writing at Ithaca College in upstate New York, and has created a documentary videotape on mothers and daughters. Her photographs of women have appeared in various feminist publications.

RUTH BABCOCK is a retired chemist, a summertime hiker, an all-the-time birder, and a sometimes writer. She lives in Oakland, CA.

WENDY TYG BATTIN graduated from Cornell University in 1975 and was a Fellow at the Fine Arts Work Center in Provincetown, MA, from 1976 to 1978. Her poems have appeared in MADEMOISELLE, EPOCH, GRANITE, and others. Currently she is a graduate student at the University of Washington in Seattle.

ROBIN BECKER (photo on page 68) lives and writes in Cambridge, MA, and teaches in the Writing Program at the Massachusetts Institute of Technology. Her poems have been published in APHRA, ASPECT, DARK HORSE, GREEN HOUSE, CHOMO-URI, and the anthology AMAZON POETRY (Out & Out Books).

RACHELLE BENVENISTE is a West Coast writer whose poety and fiction have won several prizes. She has initiated and conducted creative writing programs for children in the Culver City area and has been on the staff of the Women's Writing Conference sponsored by the International Women's Writing Guild. CEDAR ROCK, TWIGS, STONECLOUD, POETS ON, and other magazines have published her poems. "My Hair" was featured in a radio program broadcast from Station KABC in Los Angeles.

BARBARA BLOOMFIELD, born in 1954, was educated at Michigan State University, where she received her B.A. in English. She is currently living and writing in Omaha, NB.

NANCY BLOTTER grew up in Palm Springs, CA. She graduated from U.C. Berkeley and taught elementary and high school students for five years. She quit teaching in the public school system to have more time and energy for writing, and currently lives in the Santa Cruz mountains, where she waits on tables to support her poetry addiction.

LAURIE BRONSTEIN, now a student in anthropology at SUNY Binghamton, has been photographing since the age of nine (if Instamatics count).

KATHRYN CHRISTENSON, like Bernice of Fitzgerald's story, was born in Eau Claire, WI (1939) and went to the Twin Cities of Minneapolis and St. Paul for "finishing." She traded St. Paul for St. Peter (MN), and now works as teacher, administrator, and editor at Gustavus Adolphus College. Her family includes husband, son and daughter.

BARBARA CROOKER is a college teacher and a contributing editor for RIVER WORLD. Her poetry has been featured in FESTIVAL, and she was a winner in the William Carlos Williams Poetry Center's contest. Currently she lives in Fogelsville, PA, with husband Richard, daughters Stacy and Rebecca, and cat Amenhotep.

LUCILLE DAY is a graduate student in the M.A. writing program at San Francisco State University and in the Ph.D. program in science education at the University of California at Berkeley. She has two daughters. Her poetry, fiction, and non-fiction have appeared in many magazines and anthologies, such as EPOS, FICTION, POETS WEST, THE NEW YORK TIMES MAGAZINE, THE HUDSON REVIEW, and CONTEMPORARY WOMEN POETS (Merlin Press).

DIANE C. DONOVAN was born in 1956 and published her first piece of writing when she was sixteen. Primarily a poet, she is also an electric bass guitar player in a band, a cook, and a gardener.

MARCIA FALK's poems have appeared in numerous magazines and anthologies. She has published two books of translations: THE SONG OF SONGS: LOVE POEMS FROM THE BIBLE (Harcourt Brace Jovanovich, 1977) and AM I ALSO YOU? (from the Yiddish poems of Malka Heifetz—Tree Books, 1977). Having just returned from a year and a half as a postdoctoral fellow in Hebrew Literature at the Hebrew University of Jerusalem, she is an assistant professor of English and Hebrew at SUNY Binghamton.

CAROL FEWELL was born and raised in Humboldt County, CA, and moved to Berkeley in the late sixties. After an eight-year stay she moved back to Humboldt and now lives there with her daughter Caitlin while learning to listen to herself.

SIV CEDERING FOX has published her work extensively and several of her collections of poetry have been translated into other languages. Her books include MOTHER IS (Stein & Day, 1975), LETTERS FROM HELGE (New Rivers Press, 1974), COLOR POEMS (Calliopea Press, 1978), and many more. Currently she is working on several books for children as well as a novel and two more collections of poems.

ALICE FULTON (photo on page 35) has published poems in many little magazines, including DARK HORSE, THE LITTLE MAGAZINE, GREENFIELD REVIEW, and THE RUNNER. In an attempt to make poetry more accessible, she has co-authored and performed a one-act play, DANGEROUS CONVERSATIONS, which was subsequently published in WASHOUT REVIEW. Swamp Press published her collection, ANCHORS OF LIGHT in 1979. Currently she is living in New York City.

EMILIE GLEN's poems and short stories have appeared in numerous anthologies and magazines in fourteen countries, and she has received several awards for her work. She lives in New York City, where she acts in off-Broadway plays and gives frequent readings of her poems.

GAIL KADISON GOLDEN was born in July of 1943 and "grew up in too many different places to think of any one of them as home." A graduate of Barnard College and the New York University Graduate School of Social Work, she is now a psychotherapist and poet who lives in Spring Valley, NY, with her husband and two daughters.

ELIZABETH GOLDMAN is from Texas and now lives in Avon Lake, OH. Recently she received a Master's degree in Religion in Bloomington, IN.

JUDY GRAHN, author of THE WORK OF A COMMON WOMAN (Diana Press, 1978), is originally from New Mexico and currently resides in Oakland, CA, with her lover, Wendy Cadden, an artist. She is the editor of a three-volume collection of women's short stories entitled TRUE TO LIFE ADVENTURE STORIES (Diana Press). At present she is completing a matriarchal novel and history called THE MOTHERLORDS and editing four new anthologies.

JUDITH HALL (photo on page 89) lives in Lexington Park, MD.

ELLEN E. HERSH was born in New York City and raised in suburban Philadelphia. She graduated from Radcliffe College, took a M.A. in Teaching at Yale, then spent several years living in Germany and Austria, after which she taught French and German (language and literature) at the secondary and college level in the U.S. She now lives in a large converted inn in New Hampshire with her family, and participates in a workshop group consisting of poets from Massachusetts and New Hampshire.

PAULA INWOOD, after receiving her B.A. from U.C. Berkeley and her M.A. from U.C. Santa Barbara, taught English in the Fiji Islands. Currently she is the poetry specialist for the Women's History Research Center in Berkeley, works with battered wives projects in Berkeley and Santa Cruz, and teaches creative writing. Her work has appeared in MATRIX, COUNTRY WOMEN, CONCH, etc.

BILLIE JEAN JAMES has published poems in over thirty-five magazines, including SNOWY EGRET, THORN APPLE, PULP, and UNITED SISTERS. She has worked for several years as Poet in Residence for the Nevada Council on the Arts, working in the Artists in the Schools Program.

PHYLLIS JANIK, born in Chicago in May of 1944, received a B.A. from St. Xavier College and an M.F.A. from the University of Iowa. She teaches literature and creative writing at Moraine Valley College in Palos Hills, IL, and conducts readings and workshops through the Illinois Arts Council. Collections include THE DISASTER EXPERT (Basilisk, 1971), RED SHOES (Morgan Press, 1974) and AN ADVENT CALENDAR (Waxwing, 1977). "Jane" received an Illinois Literary Award.

JAN STRAUSSER KATHER was born in November of 1951. After taking a B.S. in Art Education from Edinboro State College and an M.S. in Education from Elmira College, she now works as the undergraduate photography instructor of Elmira College. She has been photographing "mirror" images since 1976.

EMILY KAY is a journalist originally from Lexington, MA, now based in Washington, DC. She has worked as a professional photographer.

JENNIFER KIDNEY was born in West Virginia in 1946, attended Oberlin and Yale (Ph.D. in English, 1974), and now works as an assistant professor of English at Oklahoma State University in Stillwater. Her poems have appeared in several little magazines.

PHYLLIS KOESTENBAUM graduated from Radcliffe College and stopped writing for twenty-five years. She recently received her M.A. in creative writing at San Francisco State University, where she won an Academy of American Poets Award. NIMROD, RESPONSE, BOTTOMFISH, CONNECTIONS, IRONWOOD and other magazines have published her work, and books are forthcoming from Jungle Garden Press and Christopher's Books.

JANE KOGAN is a professional painter who manages Provincetown Bookshop (MA) in the summer. She is in her early forties and delighted to be so.

ZANE KOTKER has extensive writing and editing experience. Knopf has published two of her novels, BODIES IN MOTION (1972) and A CERTAIN MAN (1976). Her stories, articles, and reviews have appeared in NEW YORK, RED-BOOK, THE VILLAGE VOICE, GALAXY, CROSS CURRENTS, THE NATIONAL REVIEW, and THE NEW REPUBLIC. Her current work-in-progress is a novel entitled WHITE RISING.

REBECCA KRAMER (photo on page 22) lives in Rocky Hill, NJ. where she attends junior high school. She writes poems, plays, and novellas, and last year performed a puppet play of the Rapunzel story, the opening line of which was, "Rapunzel, Rapunzel, let down your split ends!"

JOANNE LEONARD has taught at Mills College, Cornell University, and San Francisco Art Institute, and has been published in LIFE LIBRARY OF PHOTOGRAPHY and FROM THE CENTER. In 1978 she received an NEA Photo Survey grant. Her photographs have been shown across the country in numerous galleries. She is currently Assistant Professor of Art at the School of Art, University of Michigan at Ann Arbor.

LYN LIFSHIN (photo on page 30) is the editor of TANGLED VINES (Beacon Press, 1978), an anthology of mother and daughter poems. She has written over twenty-five books of poetry, including UPSTATE MADONNA, BLACK APPLES, OFFERED BY OWNER, and PLYMOUTH WOMEN. Currently she is editing an anthology of women's journal writing.

JACQUELINE LIVINGSTON, born in 1943, received her M.A. from Arizona State University. She has taught in Arizona and California, and from 1975-78 was an assistant professor at Cornell University. Her photographs have appeared in various museums across the country, and have been published in MS., ART-WEEK, VISION AND EXPRESSION (Horizon Press), and IN/SIGHTS (a collection of contemporary self-portraits by women), to name a few. SELF-PORTRAIT AS SLEEPING BEAUTY is a one-of-a-kind color-in-color print.

KAREN MARIE CHRISTA MINNS, a New Englander/upstate New Yorker now living on the West Coast, is a visual and dramatic artist as well as a poet and fiction writer. Currently she manages The Woman's Building, a public center for women's culture in Los Angeles.

HONOR MOORE's poems have been published in AMERICAN REVIEW, THE NATION, CHRYSALIS, TANGLED VINES, and other magazines and anthologies. Her verse play, MOURNING PICTURES, about her mother's death from cancer, was produced on Broadway in 1974 and published in THE NEW WOMEN'S THEATRE: TEN PLAYS BY CONTEMPORARY AMERICAN WOMEN (Vintage Books, 1977), of which she was the editor. Effie's Press has just published her chapbook, LEAVING AND COMING BACK.

RUTH MOOSE lives on an 800-acre mountain in Piedmont, NC, in a remote area noted for its abundant population of deer and rattlesnakes. She works for Poetry in the Schools in three counties. Her work has appeared in YANKEE, PRAIRIE SCHOONER, GALLIMAUFRY, and THE ATLANTIC MONTHLY, among others. In 1979 Briar Patch Press published her collection, FINDING THINGS IN THE DARK.

KATHY MORRIS (photo on page 28) lives on an organic farm in West Danby, NY. She has collaborated in numerous local publications. Her work is included in IN/SIGHTS and has appeared in MODERN PHOTOGRAPHY magazine. In the fall of 1978 she was a fellow at MacDowell Colony in Peterborough, NH.

JOYCE ODAM is poetry editor of IN A NUTSHELL. Hibiscus Press published her chapbook, LEMON CENTER FOR HOT BUTTERED ROLL, in 1975. Various magazines such as 13TH MOON, BLUE UNICORN, CIMARRON REVIEW, and CEDAR ROCK have accepted her work for publication. "The Short Hair" won a first prize in the Ina Coolbrith Circle Poetry Contest in 1975.

CHRISTINA V. PACOSZ was born in Detroit, MI, and raised by loving working class parents. She began writing early, and in 1973 moved to Oregon, where she currently works as poet-in-residence for Portland's Metro Arts Commission. SHIMMY UP TO THIS FINE MUD appeared from Poets Warehouse in 1976.

LINDA SELLERS PEAVY, a native of Mississippi, lives with her husband and two children in Bozeman, MT. Her non-fiction has appeared in professional, specialty, and inspirational magazines, and she has published four non-fiction books. "Your Uncle Will Died Today" is one of a series of stories set in the Deep South.

NAOMI RACHEL was born in California in 1952. With an M.A. in Creative Writing from San Francisco State University, she is currently living in Canada and teaching as the visiting poet at the University of British Columbia. She has over one hundred publications to her credit.

MONICA RAYMOND hails from Cambridge, MA.

BARBARA BOWN ROBINSON is a third generation Hawaiian, living in Honolulu with her family. She attended the University of Hawaii for two degrees and was the first woman to be elected president of the student government. She is a teacher, an editor, and an author of prize-winning stories, articles, and poetry. Currently she is completing a novel entitled SEVEN KAHUNA.

CHESTER SCARCE, now deceased, was the husband of Thelma Scarce.

THELMA SCARCE, (photo on page 75) a native of Colorado, received a B. A. **cum laude** in English at San Francisco State University after her children were grown. She is the fiction editor of CROW'S NEST, and her poetry has appeared in NITTY-GRITTY, CYCLO-FLAME, DRAGONFLY, and BONSAI.

JOANNE SELTZER has published poetry, fiction, and criticism. Her poems have appeared in POETRY NOW, THE MINNESOTA REVIEW, THE CIMAR-RON REVIEW, PRIMAVERA and many other literary magazines. She was one of the winners of the fifth "All Nations Poetry Contest" sponsored by Triton College in 1978. She lives in Schenectady, NY.

MAXINE SILVERMAN is the author of SURVIVAL SONG (Sunbury Press, 1976), from which the poem in this anthology is taken. Another poem from that book, "A Comfort Spell," won the Pushcart Prize and is included in PUSHCART III: BEST OF THE SMALL PRESSES.

SYBIL SMITH graduated with a B.A. in American Literature from Middlebury College. Her poems have appeared in RAINY DAY, THE GRAPEVINE, 13TH MOON, and DARK HORSE. Presently she is studying for a Master's degree in nursing at Pace University.

BARBARA SOMERS, born in 1954. was educated at Michigan State University, where she received her B.A. in English. She is currently living and writing in Omaha, NB.

BEVERLY TANENHAUS is a feminist literary critic and poet who directs the national Women's Writing Workshops in upstate New York. She is the author of TO KNOW EACH OTHER AND BE KNOWN: WOMEN'S WRITING WORKSHOPS (Out & Out Books, 1978). Her poetry is featured in CAMEOS: 12 NEW SMALL PRESS WOMEN POETS (The Crossing Press, 1978). Her feminist literary criticism has appeared in WOMEN, LITERATURE, CRITICISM (Bucknell University Press) and CHRYSALIS. Ms. Tanenhaus lives and works in Ithaca, NY.

CONCIERE TAYLOR runs and coordinates workshops, seminars, and poetry readings for the Queens Council on the Arts, and is Editor-in-Chief of SOURCE. Currently she is working on a chapbook, a trilogy of one-act plays, and a piece of fiction. THE NEW YORK TIMES, EARTH'S DAUGHTERS, WHETSTONE, WASHOUT REVIEW and others have published her work.

ROGER THORPE, who lives in Rocky Hill, NJ, is a research scientist who likes to photograph his friends.

EDITH WALDEN spent her childhood in Boise, ID, and then moved to Seattle to attend the University of Washington. While there she became seriously involved in the anti-war movement. After working as director of a large urban agriculture program for Seattle, she moved to the San Juan islands to devote full-time attention to her writing.

KATHLEENE WEST grew up in Nebraska, then moved to the Northwest, where she worked in the Poet-in-the-Schools program in Washington for two years. Currently she teaches at Olympic College, and is working on a collection of stories after the recent publication of her chapbook, NO WARNING (Jawbone Press). Since writing "Woman Combing" she has cut her hair.

Acknowledgments

"After Bernice Bobbed Her Hair" by Kathryn Christenson first appeared in the Gustavus Adolphus College FACULTY NOTES, Vol. 26, No. 8, May, 1977.

"Dead Women" by Siv Cedering Fox first appeared in MOTHER IS (Stein & Day, 1975, © Siv Cedering Fox).

"Four Views Of A Hairbrush" by Barbara Bown Robinson first appeared in THIS FRAGILE EDEN (Press Pacifica, 1979).

"Hair" p. 31 by Lyn Lifshin first appeared in UPSTATE MADONNA (Crossing Press, 1975).

"Hair" by Maxine Silverman first appeared in SURVIVAL SONG (Sunbury Press, 1976).

"A Harvest Of Unicorns" by Christina V. Pacosz first appeared in SHIMMY UP TO THIS FINE MUD (Poets Warehouse, 1976).

"Jane" by Phyllis Janik first appeared in ANOTHER CHICAGO MAGAZINE, Vol. I, Fall, 1977. The poem also received an Illinois Arts Council Literary Award.

"Jewish Wife" by Marcia Falk first appeared as a Bellevue Press poetry postcard.

"My Hair" by Katharyn Machan Aal first appeared in WAYSIDE POETRY FORUM, June, 1979.

"My Hair Is Black" by Beverly Tanenhaus first appeared in CAMEOS: 12 NEW SMALL PRESS WOMEN POETS (Crossing Press, 1978).

"My Mother's Moustache" by Honor Moore first appeared in AMERICAN REVIEW, No. 19, February, 1974.

"She Awaits His Wrath" by Wendy Tȳg Battin first appeared in GRANITE, 1977.

"The Short Hair" by Joyce Odam first appeared in BIG MOON, Vol. II, No. 2, Spring, 1976.

"Something In The Wings, The Vines" by Sybil Smith first appeared in THE GRAPEVINE, Vol. VI, No. 31, August, 1979.

"The Three Bears" by Ruth Babcock first appeared in TRUE TO LIFE ADVEN-TURE STORIES, Vol. I (Diana Press, 1978).

"Works Of Art" by Ellen E. Hersh first appeared in THE NEW HAMPSHIRE TIMES, Vol. VII, No. 4.